DO ONE GREEN THING

DO ONE GREEN THING

saving the earth through simple, everyday choices

Mindy Pennybacker

Illustrations by Carolyn Vibbert

Foreword by Meryl Streep

ST. MARTIN'S GRIFFIN ✖ NEW YORK

THOMAS DUNNE BOOKS.

AN IMPRINT OF ST. MARTIN'S PRESS.

www.thomasdunnebooks.com

www.stmartins.com

Book design by Richard Oriolo

Illustrations by Carolyn Vibbert

LIBRARY OF CONGRESS CATALOGING-IN-PUBLICATION DATA

Pennybacker, Mindy.
    Do one green thing: save the earth through simple everyday choices/Mindy Pennybacker.
        p. cm.
    Includes bibliographical references and index.
    ISBN 978-0-312-55976-2 (alk. paper)
    1. Environmentalism—Juvenile literature. 2. Environmental responsibility—Juvenile literature. I. Title.
    GE195.5.P46 2010
    333.72—dc22

                                                        2009033939

FIRST EDITION: March 2010

10 9 8 7 6 5 4 3 2 1

This book is dedicated to

Don and Rory Wallace,

stalwart green men, and the memory of

Dolly Kang Lott and Anne Wallace,

geniuses of daily life.

Contents

. . . going green can happen gradually, as we make room in our days for our individual choices.

I've always found that time and trust are of the essence in living green, especially as a working mother trying to protect children's health and the environment. Time because, although I care deeply about making the right green choices, I simply can't stop and spend an hour surfing the Web before I go shopping. Trust because it's hard to know if any source of green information that's "just out there" is up to date and practical—and not fudging the facts. Fortunately, there is now a fast and trustworthy way to find answers to the kinds of green questions I ask:

> Which products are truly healthy and green? Is there a meaningful difference between meat and dairy labeled "organic," "grass-fed," or "free range"? How can I best reduce my household's carbon footprint—without a time-consuming overhaul of my life?

> *Do One Green Thing* is for all of us who want to make good green choices without bogging ourselves down in the details. To my relief, here are the practical—and affordable—answers to all our green questions.

One green thing: It's so simple. This book takes the pressure off by giving you one easy but effective choice to make in each basic area of your life. And it's written by a trusted voice in environmental health reporting: Mindy Pennybacker. I first met Mindy as an editorial adviser to *The Green Guide*, when she became editor in chief in 1996. That she had worked at both *Glamour* magazine and the Natural Resources Defense Council attested to consumer journalism skills wedded with environmental knowledge. The first thing Mindy did as editor of *The Green Guide* was to establish a research department. With the help of the scientists on her advisory board, she made certain that all her reporting was accurate and reflected the most recent studies on a given topic, from asthma to pesticides. If you're like me, and you want to be sure that solid research informs your healthy living choices, you can rest assured that Mindy has done the work for you.

The key to making green a byword in everyone's life is ease of access: We want products we can buy and use today, without guilt and without being paralyzed by "What ifs" and "What abouts." This focus is what makes *Do One Green Thing* such a pleasure to read. It's crisp, short, visual—and there are no heavy lectures. Mindy knows we "get" green and she cuts to the chase, offering best-case answers, naming names, and providing brands. Because that's how we all shop.

With more than twenty years of environmental and green research and writing in her background, Mindy Pennybacker hasn't just jumped on the green bandwagon. *Do One Green Thing* draws on her time at *The Green Guide* and builds on her website, GreenerPenny.com, to put twenty years of consumer research at your fingertips. It breaks down essential information into clear shopping lists.

You can refer to this handy volume at the kitchen counter, on the bus or train, or in store aisles. For those who want a little more back story, each chapter includes the latest science on how your choice relates to your personal health and the environment. Like a lot of people, I first came to green living as a parent. When our children are born, we want to protect them and nurture them: When it comes to additives in food, or exposure to toxic chemicals in toys and furnishings, or to polluted air and water, parents are the front line of defense for our children and our homes. As a parent, Mindy understands this and focuses on the risks that we can control, with a minimum of effort and anxiety. She also understands that life is not all about being green. We all do what we can; *Do One Green Thing* is here to help us do more, without stressing ourselves needlessly.

As I have found in my own life, going green can happen gradually, as we make room in our days for our individual choices—and pleasures. And so Mindy doesn't sternly command us to get rid of that favorite little beauty secret, even if it does contain some less-than-ideal ingredients. One little dab a day isn't going to do you in. What matters is that we reduce our overall exposures to iffy chemicals over time, and there's plenty of opportunity to do this in our choice of alternative cosmetics, home products, and food. And thanks to our consumer demand, before we know it there might just be perfect green versions of our favorite little beauty secrets, too.

It feels so right to be reading this book, by this author, at this time. More than a dozen years ago, when I was on the board of Mothers and Others for a Livable Planet, the nonprofit organization that supported sustainable agriculture and published *The Green Guide*, Mindy and I were both reading books by small family farmers about the nearly insurmountable hardships they faced. Today, with the growth of demand for organic, local, and heritage foods, there is hope, not only for independent farmers but for all of us.

Do One Green Thing makes me feel happy and confident that more positive change is afoot, and that we all have an important and rewarding part to play.

—MERYL STREEP

. . . an environmentally responsible life is above all meant to be enjoyed.

If you can read and reference only one green thing, make it this book. All the basics you need to know are right here at your fingertips. When you wonder if it's worth switching to a green detergent, what kind of plastic your sports bottle is made of, or which fish is safest to eat, look no further. This book is for the person who doesn't do or buy everything green, but who wants to make a difference where it matters. In other words, it's for all of us.

All around us, a new green world is opening up and sending forth shoots. Thanks to consumer and political pressure, toxic chemicals have been banned from children's toys, and companies are cleaning up their products and processes. Yes, the globe is still experiencing warming, among other problems, and we aren't going to solve it all overnight. But by doing simple things in our daily lives, such as voting with our wallets for greener products, we are collectively making a difference.

We now understand that our personal health and the health of our planet are inextricably linked, and that's enough to give anyone eco-anxiety. While chemicals in pesticides, plastics, household cleaners, and cosmetics are causing harm to wildlife and collecting in our bodies, global warming is being linked to the spread of disease and to extreme weather, which can cause crop failure and famine.

Naturally, for many of us, the idea that both our bodies and our planet may be in peril is downright frightening, if not paralyzing. This book is here to reassure you.

We often feel that if we aren't ready or able to make radical, self-sacrificing change, then we may as well not even try. What good will it do? The answer: a lot.

Some of the most valuable advice I've received has come from Meryl Streep, who was a member of the editorial advisory board at a publication I edited called *The Green Guide*. A strong supporter of children's health and informed consumer choices in the marketplace, Meryl reminded me to be positive and to focus in this book on the simple ways we can help solve environmental problems, so that readers don't panic and just give up. A green life, like any life, is a work in progress, and most of us aren't ready for an extreme makeover, which usually involves a major commitment of money and time. So if you want to change, step by step, in ways that really make a difference, where to begin?

This book is here to help you take the first (and most efficient) steps, by providing the one affordable green thing you can do in the basic areas of your daily life: water, food, home, work, personal care, and apparel. It makes sense to start with the kinds of food and other products your household consumes most, the way you use the greatest amount of electricity and water and what health concerns, if any, are important to you. Got allergies but can't afford an all-organic mattress? A tightly woven case over your old one will keep chemicals and dust mites at bay. Worried about your drinking water? Municipal water is actually more strictly regulated than bottled, and comes without the severe environmental cost of plastic. When in doubt, a pitcher with a carbon filter will protect you from most common contaminants.

This book is full of such simple tips. In more than a decade of editing green lifestyle publications and websites, from *The Green Guide* to GreenerPenny.com, the question I've heard most frequently from readers is "If I can do only one thing green (in my diet, kitchen, cleaning, cosmetics, baby's room), what should it be?" This book provides the answers to that question.

For me, making positive, realistic change—such as buying hormone-free milk for my child or keeping pesticides out of our home—was not only empowering, but it also made the fear go away. And that's where the seed of this book began: I wanted to present information about going green in a way that would make it easy for people to incorporate changes no matter what stage they were currently at.

One green thing multiplied by the many of us willing to make the effort can add up to a big difference. For example, in 2008, in response to our demand for fresh local food, the number of U.S. farmers' markets reached 4,685, a nearly 7 percent increase in two years. Voting with our wallets is stimulating double-digit growth in organic and fairly traded food and natural personal care products. But because "natural" claims aren't always meaningful, this book will help you choose products that are truly green, rather than pay extra for "greenwashing" hype.

Over the years, I've learned a lot from my readers, who have busy lives and are far more interested in practical tips than doom-and-gloom. An environmentally responsible life is above all meant to be enjoyed. Green innovation is happening in energy and electronics, fashion and beauty, children's products, home decoration and entertaining—which are often beautifully designed and carry all the more cachet for their planet-protecting (and sometimes money-saving) features. Now, rather than spending time trying to figure out how best to go green, you can simply use that time to make the difference.

. . . with these affordable everyday choices and small changes in our habitual behaviors, the cumulative effect will be monumental.

The book is divided into four sections, which are then broken into thirteen chapters. These divisions reflect the areas where we can make the most difference—for ourselves and the planet. With these affordable everyday choices and small changes in our habitual behaviors, the cumulative effect will be monumental.

Each chapter is organized around a few basic issues. Inside each, you'll find:

ONE GREEN THING. Each chapter begins with a simple idea: If you could do One Green Thing that related to the given topic, what would it be? I provide a single, straightforward suggestion. (Example: When it comes to produce, buy locally grown fruits and vegetables.)

MOST-ASKED QUESTION. The bulk of each chapter will be devoted to answering the questions that I'm most frequently asked. (Example: Which plastic product contains the least amount of toxic chemicals?)

CHOOSE IT/LOSE IT. The choices in this two-column list specify, in detail, the answers to the most-asked questions. There I explain which green choice you should make, and which non-green choice to avoid, with a brief explanation of the rationale. (Example: If you can't afford to buy all organic, choose organic spinach but not organic broccoli, since regular broccoli doesn't have high levels of pesticide residue.)

Regarding your green choices, a section called **The Science** will briefly explain why this choice is greener and in what ways it is:

BETTER FOR YOUR HEALTH: a brief, simple explanation of the science behind why to make this choice for your better health;

BETTER FOR THE PLANET: a simple explanation of why to make this choice for the sake of the global environment; and

BETTER FOR SOCIAL JUSTICE: when farm communities and worker welfare benefit from green initiatives.

There are also useful boxes and sidebars distributed throughout. A few examples include:

SAMPLE SHOPPING LISTS

GREENERPENNY'S TOP PICKS: what gives good value for your budget, for your health, and for the Earth

TRULY GREEN LABELS VS. "GREENWASHING" LABELS

INGREDIENTS TO LOOK FOR/AVOID

To see illustrations of recommended seals and labels, turn to the Resources section at the back of the book, where you'll also find listings of green organizations and their websites. End notes keyed to each chapter provide full research sources for the studies and other facts reported in the book.

The comprehensive product lists, tips, and sources in this book should provide you with all you need, in one handy and well-organized place, to make all your daily green living choices. For news and updates on all these topics, or if you've any questions or feedback for me, please visit www.greenerpenny.com.

I. Food and Drink

. . . if just one out of twenty
Americans stopped buying water
in disposable bottles, we'd save
30 million pounds of plastic
waste a year.

ONE GREEN THING

Free yourself from the bottled water habit.

Why? If every American stopped buying water in disposable bottles:

1. We'd save the nonrenewable fossil fuels that are used in the plastic, which equals seventeen million barrels of oil annually—enough to fuel one million U.S. cars for a year. Adding in the energy used for pumping, processing, transporting, and refrigerating bottled water, Americans would save fifty-four million barrels of oil, the same as running three million cars for a year.

2. We'd save greenhouse gas emissions by keeping at least 2.5 million tons of CO_2 out of the atmosphere.

3. We'd save water. Bottled water has a heavy water footprint: Twice as much water goes into making a bottle as its contents, so every bottle of water sold actually represents *three* bottles of water.

4. We'd save energy. Bottled water uses more energy than tap—up to two thousand times more, depending on the distance it travels to the consumer.

5. We'd save money. Worldwide, every year, an estimated $100 billion is spent on bottled water. If you replace just one bottle of store-bought water ($1.50 and up for 12 ounces) a day with tap water (less than $0.10 per gallon) you'll save at least $440 a year.

most-asked question

Isn't bottled spring water safer than tap water?

Not necessarily. Tests of bottled water have found many unhealthy contaminants.

DRINKING WATER

choose it

Drink tap water. Fill your own reusable bottle.

lose it

Don't drink bottled water, except when you really need it. For example, local reservoirs may be contaminated after a storm, or you may be traveling in places that don't have safe public water supplies.

better for your health

Be assured that most water in the United States, both bottled and tap, is safe to drink, although there are periodic public alerts of contamination by lead, chemicals, or bacteria. Bottled water, though, is actually *less* strictly regulated than tap. Tests of 10 mainstream brands of bottled water by the Environmental Working Group in 2008, and of 103 brands by the Natural Resources Defense Council in 1999, found bacteria and toxic chemicals in many of the samples. Because public water supplies are regulated, you can easily find out if your tap water contains unhealthy contaminants, most of which can be painlessly removed by using refillable pitchers and faucet attachments with replaceable carbon filter cartridges by makers such as Brita, Pur, and Zero Water.

better for the planet

To top off all the savings already mentioned, if just one out of twenty Americans stopped buying water in disposable bottles, we'd save 30 million pounds of plastic waste a year. Although they're recyclable, more than 80 percent of plastic water bottles in the United States end up in landfills. Tapping into springs, whether in the United States, France, or Fiji, can cause lower water flow and the drying up of creek beds, which harms ecosystems downstream.

better for social justice

At present, 1.1 billion of the world's people, mostly the poor, do not have access to safe drinking water. When private companies take and bottle spring (or even tap) water—often for little to no money paid to local communities—they endanger the political stability of poor countries and the health of residents who can't afford to pay for clean tap water. By choosing public tap water over private bottled water, we're helping buck the creeping trend toward treating clean water as a market commodity rather than a service that all governments should provide.

WHAT'S IN YOUR

By July 1 of every year, your water utility company is required to send you a report listing any contaminants in your water supply that exceed EPA safety levels. If you don't receive your report in the mail, call the utility to request it, or check for it online at the Environmental Working Group's national tap water database: www.ewg.org/tapwater/yourwater/
or at www.epa.gov/safewater/dwinfo/index.html.

Consumers Union rates carbon filter performance at **www.greenerchoices.org/ratings. cfm?product=waterfilter.**

Finding the Right Filter

Regular carbon filters, like those in carafes or faucet attachments, remove heavy metals such as lead and arsenic, some parasites such as cryptosporidium and giardia, pesticides, and other toxic chemicals. But carbon filters do not remove bacteria, which may enter systems after storms and sewage spills. In the case of local drinking water alerts, drink bottled water (purified water is cheap) and consider ways to further clean up your tap water if contamination continues.

For how-tos on filtering bacteria and other contaminants, go to **www.nrdc.org/water/drinking/gfilters.asp.**

WATER?

Worth a Test: Lead

Lead may also enter your water through old lead-lined water mains and building pipes. If you're pregnant or have young children, it's a good idea to use a carbon filter as a precaution while you have your tap water tested for lead. Ask your city department of health or environmental protection agency if they provide free water testing. If not, find a nearby certified testing lab at www.epa.gov/safewater/labs/index.html.

Recycling Carbon Filters

Preserve Products recycles Brita pitcher filters, which can be dropped off at many Whole Foods stores. See www.preserveproducts.com/recycling/britafilters.html.

You can also mail filters to Brita and to Zero Water for recycling (but you pay for the postage). Zero Water will reward you with discounts on new filters. See www.zerowater.com.

WATER BOTTLES

most-asked question

I've heard that some plastic bottles leach toxic chemicals. What's the safest reusable water bottle?

Choose reusable bottles made from safe plastic or stainless steel.

FINDING A SAFE BOTTLE FOR YOUR TAP WATER

choose it

Choose reusable drink bottles made from the following materials:

1. Stainless-steel beverage bottles

2. Tempered glass baby bottles

3. Bottles specifically made to be reused, crafted out of plastics that have not been found to leach toxic chemicals:

   - High-density polyethylene (HDPE #2)

   - Low-density polyethylene (LDPE #4)

   - Polypropylene (PP #5)

   - Tritan copolyester (Other #7), a new transparent plastic that the manufacturer assures is made without BPA

lose it

Lose the following:

1. Bottles made with polycarbonate (PC #7),* also known as Lexan, which can release toxic Bisphenol A (BPA) into their contents (see "Plastics by the Numbers" on page 10.)

2. Reusing disposable plastic water or juice bottles made of polyethylene (PET, or PETE, #1) more than once or twice

*Some baby bottles are also made of PC.

the science

better for your health

By not drinking out of PC bottles, you'll avoid one major risk of exposure to a chemical called Bisphenol A (BPA), which the U.S. National Toxicology Center has warned may interfere with normal human brain and hormonal development. BPA crosses the placenta, and thus also poses a particular threat to fetuses; it also can harm young children. "I would advise a pregnant woman to try to reduce or entirely eliminate her exposure to Bisphenol A," said the lead author of a 2009 study. Higher levels of BPA have been implicated in cardiovascular disease and diabetes in adults. For more information, see the "Food Storage and Cookware" chapter, starting on page 65.

By not reusing disposable bottles, you'll avoid possible illness from the bacteria that they collect, even when washed. Unlike wide-mouth sports bottles that are easy to clean, disposables are not made to be reused. Most disposable water bottles are made of very thin polyethylene (PET #1) plastic; hormone-imitating chemicals have been found in water from some samples of PET bottles, including some that have been stored for long periods, or at high temperatures (often attained when left in a car or backpack in the sun). PET is also the most recyclable plastic, so feel good about tossing these disposables in a recycling bin rather than reusing.

better for the planet

Choosing non-BPA plastics sends a strong message to companies to decrease the manufacture of this toxic chemical and its release into the environment.

Still, more and more kinds of disposable water bottles are being made. PET #1, while easily recyclable, is made from petroleum, a nonrenewable resource whose massive carbon and water footprints are noted above.

Another new kind of plastic bottle on the market is made out of polylactide (PLA #7) bioplastics. PLA, a clear plastic made from corn or potato starch, is not readily recyclable—but if the occasional PLA bottle gets tossed in a recycle bin, it won't cause harm. Overall, bioplastics are greener than conventional plastics,

PLASTICS BY

You can usually identify plastics by the recycling code numbers in the "chasing arrows" triangle stamped on the bottom of the containers. Refer to this list for the environmental and health impacts of different plastics, listed here:

- **#1 polyethylene terephthalate (PET, or PETE):** It is used in most disposable and some sports bottles, is easily recyclable, but, alas, seldom recycled. (Ninety percent of disposable water bottles wind up in landfills, according to the Container Recycling Institute.) It does not leach BPA, but may, in rare instances, leach other chemicals if heated or old.

- **#2 high-density polyethylene (HDPE):** It is used in milk and gallon water jugs, is the most widely recycled plastic, and has not been found to leach any chemicals.

- **#3 polyvinyl chloride (PVC):** The worst plastic in my book and the least recyclable, it can leach toxic lead and phthalates, plasticizing chemicals that have been linked to the development of irregular reproductive organs in male infants and obesity in men.

since they're made from renewable plant materials rather than petroleum. For more info on bioplastics, which are also used to make food containers, see "Food Storage and Cookware," page 71.

THE NUMBERS

- #4 low-density polyethylene (LDPE): This is a somewhat recyclable plastic that hasn't been found to leach.

- #5 polypropylene (PP): Not easily recycled, but popular in reusable bottles and food containers, it hasn't been found to leach chemicals into water.

- #6 polystyrene (PS): Another baddie, used in Styrofoam cups/containers and also some clear containers and eating utensils; it can leach styrene, a cancer-causing chemical, especially when heated.

- #7 "other" (a catch-all number, when referring to polycarbonate [PC]): This leaches BPA.

- #7 "other" (when applied to copolyester (Tritan): It has not been found to leach BPA, but is also not recyclable.

- #7 "other" (for bioplastics): Made from plants, not fossil fuels, this has not been found to leach chemicals, but is unfortunately neither recyclable nor very reusable, and will properly biodegrade only in an industrial composting facility.

GreenerPenny's Tip

BETTER BOTTLES SHOPPING LIST

No need to toss a perfectly good new PC sports bottle! Use it with care and hand-wash it rather than in the dishwasher. (Bottles that have been heavily used, scratched, or submitted to high heat are more likely leach BPA.) When your bottle shows signs of wear, replace it with a BPA-free stainless-steel or plastic model from the following list:

TOP PICKS: LIGHTWEIGHT, UNLINED STAINLESS-STEEL BOTTLES

Bilt (www.ems.com)

Enviro Products (www.enviroproductsinc.com)

Guyot Backpacker (www.guyotdesigns.com)

Klean Kanteen (www.kleankanteen.com)

Riverkeeper (www.riverkeeper.org)

Thermos makes water bottles as well as its trademark insulated bottles (www.shopthermos.com)

Reusable glass has its fans, too. A long-necked glass bottle with an attached rubber and ceramic stopper is sold at www.livinglavidaverde.net/store.aspx

BETTER PLASTIC WATER BOTTLES

Camelbak Tritan (www.rei.com)

Nalgene Tritan, or HDPE #2 (www.rei.com)

Novara PET #1 (www.rei.com)

Rubbermaid Chug Sport, Sippin' Sport, PP #5 (www.target.com or www.amazon.com)

Somafab PP #5 (www.somafab.com)

Tupperware tumblers, PP #5 (www.tupperware.com)

BEST BABY BOTTLES (NON-PC PLASTIC, OR GLASS WHERE NOTED)

Adiri (www.babybungalow.com)

Bornfree (glass) (www.newbornfree.com)

Dr. Brown's (www.handi-craft.com)

Evenflo Classics (glass) (www.ingeling.com)

Gerber Fashion Tints and Clear View (www.amazon.com)

Green to Grow (www.greentogrow.com)

Medela breast milk storage and feeding set (www.target.com)

Playtex (www.playtexbaby.com)

Sassy MAM (www.mambabyusa.com)

WATER BOTTLES WITH BUILT-IN WATER FILTERS

When used according to instructions, the following portable, non-leaching plastic bottles will remove bacteria and viruses. Great for backpackers or for use in emergencies.

Aquamira Water Bottle with Microbiological Filter (www.aquamira.com)

Fit and Fresh LivPure (www.target.com)

Katadyn Micro Water Bottle (www.rei.com)

WaterGeeks (www.thewatergeeks.com)

For more information, log on to www.greenerpenny.com.

Buy organic for those

foods you and your family

eat most.

Produce 2

ONE GREEN THING

Choose organic and locally grown produce.

Why: Organic agriculture greatly reduces exposures to pesticides in your body and the environment; buying locally preserves small farms and green space.

I've always tried to eat lots of fresh vegetables and fruits, but it wasn't until I became a mother that organic produce became part of our daily life. When our child was two years old and entering preschool, I read a report that young children were being exposed to high levels of dangerous pesticides in their food. What could parents do to protect their children? We didn't want to stop feeding them vegetables and fruit. Did peeling remove pesticides? No. Could we substitute pears for apples? No. Consumer Reports tests showed that pears had high levels, too.

The solution: Organic produce was grown without these pesticides. Money was tight, but my husband and I decided that we would buy organic apples and pears, our child's favorite fruits.

BENEFITS OF ORGANIC PRODUCE

most-asked question

For the sake of my budget and my health, which fruits and veggies are most important to buy organic?

Buy organic for those foods you and your family eat most. It is also worthwhile to buy the organic version of produce known to have high pesticide residues. You can economize by not spending the extra on organic for things you eat only once in a while, or for the Tasty Thirteen (see the "Choose It/Lose It" table, at right), which have the very lowest levels of pesticide residue.

WHEN TO BUY ORGANIC

👍 *choose it*

Buy the organic version of the produce you and your family eat the most.

The Toxic Thirteen: You may also want to buy organic in the following foods, which otherwise have the highest pesticide residues:

Apples	Nectarines
Carrots	Peaches
Celery	Pears
Cherries	Spinach
Grapes	Strawberries
Kale	Sweet bell peppers
Lettuce	

👎 *lose it*

Buy non-organic in foods you eat only once in a while, or those having the lowest pesticide residues.

The Tasty Thirteen listed here are generally low in pesticides and okay to buy non-organic.

Asparagus	Pineapple
Avocadoes	Sweet corn
Broccoli	Sweet peas
Cabbage	Sweet potatoes
Eggplant	Tomatoes
Mango	Watermelon
Onion	

Which had the very lowest number of pesticides? The lowly onion!

Source: Adapted from the Environmental Working Group's 2009 *Shopper's Guide to Pesticides* and rankings of forty-seven fruits and vegetables. For the full list, go to www.foodnews.org.

HOW WILL I KNOW IF IT'S ORGANIC?

For whole, unprocessed foods—produce, meat, dairy—it's simple. Look for the label "USDA Certified Organic."

Organic means less exposure to risky pesticides. While it is impossible to avoid all harmful toxins, if you're mindful, you can cut down on your exposure to harmful substances. About 940 million pounds of pesticides are applied to U.S. crops a year, and 40 percent of these chemicals are linked to cancer or nervous system harm. In order to qualify for "USDA Organic" certification, food must be grown without synthetic pesticides or fertilizers. And based on USDA data, scientists at Consumers Union, the publisher of Consumer Reports, have determined that organic produce has two-thirds less pesticide residue than average produce does.

Why are organic fruits and vegetables only two-thirds free of pesticide residue instead of 100 percent clean? Pesticides drift in the air and contaminate soil and water, persisting in the environment and our bodies for years. Although DDT was banned in the United States in the 1970s, it's still found in everything from Inuit mother's milk and the blubber of marine mammals to spinach and red-backed salamanders. That's why, although farm fields are required to be free of all synthetic pesticide applications for three years before their produce can be labeled "USDA Organic," persistent pesticide residue in the soil can result in traces in organically grown food.

Young children can easily be exposed through food to unsafe levels of pesticides that are linked to learning and behavioral problems, studies by the Environmental Working Group have shown.

> The lead researcher in the 2007 UK comparison study equated eating organic with consuming an extra portion of produce a day.

Organic may give a nutrition boost: The biggest comparison study between organic and conventionally grown produce to date, conducted in Britain in 2007, concluded that organic produce has 40 percent higher levels of cancer-fighting antioxidants.

Organic are the only foods certifiably free of genetic engineering or modification.

better for the planet

Organic agriculture forbids the use of synthetic chemicals, meaning those that are man-made, mostly from fossil fuels such as petroleum and natural gas. Avoiding the use of such synthetic pesticides and fertilizers protects the environment in several ways:

- We cut down on consumption of fossil fuels.
- We cut down on global warming gases.
- We prevent the harm they do to plants and wildlife.

Pesticides contaminate the soil and water, spread in the air, and kill birds, fish, amphibians, and beneficial insects such as honeybees. Synthetic nitrogen fertilizers oversaturate the soil and run off into waterways, causing increased proliferation of algae, which results in oxygen depletion, fish kills, and oceanic dead zones.

Organic farmers are not permitted to use genetically engineered seeds (see Glossary). Genetically engineered crops—corn, soy, cotton, and canola—threaten seed diversity, because their pollen has been found to drift, spreading these genes to other plants. The damage is the dilution of the diversity of crops, which are humankind's seed banks against famine. Crops that have been genetically engineered have also contaminated organic crops through pollen drift, causing organic farmers to lose their certification. There are now fears that the spread of genetically engineered herbicide-resistance pollen may lead to the development of super weeds.

ORGANIC FARMING METHODS BENEFIT THE EARTH

- They enrich the soil with compost, nourishing microorganisms and earthworms, which naturally make the soil fertile.
- The planting of cover crops and leaving areas of forest and native vegetation standing (two organic farming methods) prevent soil erosion; this also protects water sources.

BENEFITS OF LOCALLY GROWN FOOD

Buying food that was grown within 100 to 200 miles of where it's sold (the criteria for inclusion in most farmers' markets) cuts down on greenhouse gas emissions and air pollution from the fossil fuels burned in transporting the food long distances. Local produce is also usually sold by smaller, diversified farms that grow a variety of crops. This provides an important counterbalance to the growth of large, industrial organic farms that grow only one crop and distribute nationwide to large food processors and retailers.

In Iowa alone, non-local produce travels an estimated 1,500 miles from farm to plate (versus the 56 miles for locally grown food), using about four times as much fuel and releasing four times as much greenhouse gas, according to a 2001 study by the Leopold Institute for Sustainable Agriculture at Iowa State University.

another question

Is it better to buy local or organic?

The answer's simple. Buy both!

Michael Pollan, bestselling author of *The Omnivore's Dilemma* and *In Defense of Food,* says he prefers local, organically grown food from farmers' markets, even if it's not certified organic, a label that many small farmers can't afford. At the farmers' market, he points out, you can simply ask the farmer if pesticides were used. Still, local and organic are both good and should therefore not be viewed as mutually exclusive.

QUESTIONS TO ASK AT THE FARMERS' MARKET

- Do you use synthetic pesticides or fertilizers?

- Do you use genetically engineered seed?

- What measures do you take to protect soil quality, wildlife habitat, and watersheds?

In a growing online network, you can also chat with food producers from dairy farmers and cheesemakers to chocolatiers, and order their wares, on websites such as www.foodzie.com.

HOW CAN I TELL WHERE A FRUIT OR VEGETABLE COMES FROM?

If you find it at a farmers' market, it comes from within 200 miles of the market.

If you're shopping at a supermarket, produce must have a "country of origin label" (COOL), to indicate if it comes from the United States or abroad. But within the United States, there's no law requiring identification of the state or region where the produce was grown, so look for labels or signs, or simply ask the produce manager where that apple, kale, or arugula hails from.

GOOD GREEN PRODUCE LABELS AND WHAT THEY MEAN

Here are some of the labels you might find on fresh produce, and a key to what they mean.*

DEMETER BIODYNAMIC: This holistic label indicates that the methods used to grow the produce fulfill all organic requirements and beyond, treat the Earth as a living organism, take care to protect wild flora and fauna, and strive for a light carbon footprint (www.demeter-usa.org).

FAIR TRADE CERTIFIED (TRANSFAIR USA): Applies the strictest standards, ensuring that farmers receive fair prices and that workers receive fair wages and health protections during the cultivation of coffee, tea, chocolate, tropical fruit, rice, sugar, honey (www.transfairusa.org).

FOOD ALLIANCE CERTIFIED: Uses IPM and also protects worker and animal welfare (www.foodalliance.org).

INTEGRATED PEST MANAGEMENT (IPM): Synthetic pesticides are used only as a last resort, and then sparingly, relying on nontoxic methods and beneficial insects that eat pests. See Consumers Union's www.greenerchoices.org, and www.ipminstitute.org/for the best IPM labels, such as Protected Harvest.

RAINFOREST ALLIANCE CERTIFIED: Guarantees that tropical produce (bananas, oranges, pineapples, passion fruit), and coffee, tea, and chocolate, are grown with IPM in ways that conserve rainforests and protect workers' health (www.ra.org).

* For illustrations of the above seals, see Resources.

SALMON SAFE: Indicates that the produce is either organic or IPM, and is grown using methods that protect western watersheds and rivers from runoff (www.salmonsafe.org).

TRANSITIONAL ORGANIC: In some states, farmers using verified organic methods may use this label until they've met the three-year requirement for USDA Organic labeling. By telling consumers their products are grown without synthetic pesticides, this label can be a lifesaver for farmers going through the expensive, complex conversion process.

USDA ORGANIC: Last but far from least, this label sets the clearest and most reliable standard for produce grown in environmentally safe and sound ways. It indicates that no synthetic (man-made) pesticides or fertilizers were used; sewage sludge was not applied to the fields; and no genetic engineering or irradiation took place (www.ams.usda.gov/NOP).

GOOD NEWS!

Organic remains the fastest-growing sector of the food industry. Over the past twenty years, it has expanded at 22–23 percent annually, compared with 2–3 percent for the industry as a whole. By 2008, locally grown produce had become one of the fastest-growing segments of the agricultural market.

SEASONAL EATING

Tip: Eat fresh produce in season. It's much less confusing than worrying about "food miles," a varying and uncertain equation at best. Some argue that the calculation of food miles should factor in the means of transportation (shipping by boat, for instance, emits less CO_2 than by truck or plane), and how the food is produced. If it's grown in a heated greenhouse in winter, then it's local, but not in season. Seasonal eating helps you avoid the greenhouse gas trap in more ways than one.

To find out what's in season in your locale, and where to get it: Click on your state at Sustainable Table's helpful "Eat Seasonal" page, which shows both the harvest season and availability of most varieties of fresh fruits and vegetables **(www.sustainabletable.org/shop/eatseasonal/).**

Go to the farmers' market and see what's there. To find a farmers' market near you, go to www.localharvest.org or www.apps.ams.usda.gov/FarmersMarkets/.

No farmers' market near you? Try a farm stand or a pick-your-own farm, which you can search for under "farms" and "direct marketing" at **www.localharvest.org or www.pickyourown.org.** *It also indicates which farms are organic.*

LOOKING AHEAD: A LABEL TO HOPE FOR

A label certifying products of family farms grown with environmental and fair labor standards is being developed by the Association of Family Farms and the National Farmers' Union (www.nfu.org).

IS ORGANIC JUNK FOOD BETTER?

another question

Aren't organic chips and cookies healthier for my family than non-organic versions?

Not necessarily! Although pesticide residues don't survive food processing, organic junk food is still junk food, says Marion Nestle, New York University nutrition professor and author of *What to Eat* and *Food Politics*. In other words, organic snacks are just as fattening.

You still have to read labels. For example, some 100 percent organic peanut butters contain organic sugar and organic palm oil. While these ingredients have been grown and processed according to organic standards, and are thus better for the environment, they're still unnecessary added sugars and fats. Organic white flour is still white flour; whole wheat, organic or not, is better because of the fiber and vitamins it naturally packs.

HOW ORGANIC IS AN "ORGANIC" CEREAL OR OTHER PROCESSED FOOD?

It's all too easy to grab a package of cereal or macaroni and cheese that bears the word "organic," but isn't authentically so. Here's how to make sure you get the real thing.

100% ORGANIC: Made with all certified organic ingredients (excluding salt and water); displays USDA Organic label.

ORGANIC: At least 95 percent organic ingredients; displays USDA Organic label.

MADE WITH ORGANIC: At least 70 percent organic ingredients; may not display USDA Organic label, but may list up to three organic ingredients on front of package.

Processed foods containing less than 70 percent organic ingredients may not display organic claims on the front of their package; they can list their organic ingredients on their information/ingredient panel only.

Organic means less exposure to risky pesticides.

*For pictures of above seals, see Resources.

COFFEE, TEA, AND CHOCOLATE

Most of us don't want to avoid these guilty pleasures, which are easily found in green varieties. What's greenest? Choose coffee, tea, or a chocolate bar that bears as many of the following labels as possible*:

BIRD-FRIENDLY: The coffee has been certified as "shade-grown" by the Smithsonian Migratory Bird Center (www.nationalzoo.si.edu). The crops are cultivated in the rainforest, under the natural canopies, the way they originated. (In the 1960s, forests were cleared for higher-yield "sun" plantations that depended on pesticides.) In shade growing, leaf litter on the forest floor provides natural fertilizer and protects against pests and disease. A 2008 study found that "Bird-Friendly" farms had more than twice as many forest birds in residence as other farms.

CERTIFIED ORGANIC: The crop is grown without any synthetic pesticides or fertilizers, using cover crops and other methods to protect soil fertility.

FAIR TRADE CERTIFIED: The coffee, tea, or cacao was bought directly from farmer cooperatives at prices higher than the commodity market rate, and grown using IPM methods, including shade cultivation. The use of hazardous pesticides, such as DDT, methyl parathion, and lindane, is not permitted—period (www.transfairUSA.org).

RAINFOREST ALLIANCE CERTIFIED: RA standards protect workers' rights and welfare, ensuring that they receive at least the local minimum wage; forbid child labor; and require that at least 40 percent of the plantation be grown in forest shade. Many pesticides, including those on the Pesticide Action Network's "Dirty Dozen" list, are banned by RA (www.ra.org).

COFFEE, TEA, AND CHOCOLATE

BEST COFFEE SHOPPING LIST

The coffees listed here get three stars: They're certified Organic, Fair Trade, and labeled either Bird-Friendly or Rainforest Alliance.

Arbuckle "Organic Line" (www.arbucklecoffee.com)

Audubon Breakfast Blend (www.auduboncoffeeclub.com)

Bisbee (www.bisbeecoffee.com)

Café Canopy (www.cafecanopy.com)

Café Ibis (www.cafeibis.com)

Café Moto (www.cafemoto.com)

Caribou (www.cariboucoffee.com)

Catskill Mountain (www.catskillmountaincoffee.com)

Coffee AM (www.coffeeam.com)

Deans Beans Birdwatchers Blend (www.deansbeans.com)

Elan Organic (www.elanorganic.com)

Higher Ground (www.highergroundroasters.com)

Jim's Organic (www.jimsorganiccoffee.com)

Marques de Paiva (www.marquesdepaiva.com)

Montana Coffee Traders (www.coffeetraders.com)

BEST TEA SHOPPING LIST

The following teas are certified fairly traded (FT), organic (O), or both (FT/O).

Choice Organic (FT/O): Their flavors really pop. Try Moroccan Mint and Mango Ceylon (www.choiceorganicteas.com).

Equal Exchange (FT/O): They stock classics such as Darjeeling; and old/new choices such as Rooibos (www.equalexchange.org).

Guayaki Organic Yerba Mate (FT/O: Comes in both tea bags and as a bottled drink. Yerba Mate is a powerful caffeinated pick-me-up (www.guayaki.com).

Honest Tea (O): President Obama has stocked the White House fridge with these bottled teas, especially in his favorite Green Dragon and Black Forest Berry flavors (www.honesttea.com).

Steenbergs (FT/O): They carry authentic loose-leaf English Breakfast and Earl Grey teas (www.Steenbergs.co.uk).

BEST CHOCOLATE SHOPPING LIST

There's been a lot of controversy in the past few years over the use of child slavery on cacao plantations. The following companies sell chocolate that's Fair Trade or Rainforest Alliance (RA) Certified, both of which require that the chocolate be grown without forced child labor. The Rainforest Alliance (RA) and the Fair Trade Federation (FTF) also protect workers and ensure sustainable agriculture standards. If products are also organic, they get an (O).

Art Bar (O) (www.artbar.com)

Cocavino (O) (www.cocoavino.com)

Divine (www.divinechocolate.com)

Eccobella (www.eccobella.com)

Equal Exchange (O) (www.equalexchange.org)

Gaia (O) (www.katescaringgifts.com)

Green and Black's Maya Gold bars (O) (www.greenandblacks.com)

Grounds for Change (www.groundsforchange.com)

Lake Champlain Hot Cocoa (O) (www.lakechamplainchocolates.com)

La Siembra (www.lasiembra.com)

Newman's Own Organics (O) (www.newmansownorganics.com)

Rapunzel (O) (www.rapunzel.com)

Sweet Earth (O) (www.sweetearthchocolates.com)

Theo's (O): Proceeds from their Jane Goodall Bar contribute to Goodall's institute's work to protect chimpanzees (www.theochocolate.com)

Vintage Plantations Arriba (www.chocolatepath.com)

Yachana (www.yachanagourmet.com)

For more information, log on to www.greenerpenny.com.

ALCOHOL
Wine

Drinking wine in moderation—say, one 5-ounce glass a day—is good for the heart. But people with asthma and allergies may breathe easier drinking USDA-certified organic wine, which forbids the addition of sulfites, a common allergen. (European organic wines do allow added sulfites, although in lower levels than in non-organic varieties.)

GreenerPenny's
BEST WINES SHOPPING LIST

Here are some organic (O) and biodynamic (B) vintages, as well eco-label wines such as Salmon Safe and LIVE (an Oregon certification based on controlling pests with beneficial insects rather than pesticides), and where they're made.

Amity Vineyards (O): Oregon (www.amityvineyards.com)

Badger Mountain Vineyard (O): Washington State (www.badgermountainvineyard.com)

Bonterra Vineyards (O): California (www.bonterra.com)

Brickhouse Wines (O): Oregon (www.brickhousewines.com)

Ceago Vinegarden (O/B): California (www.ceago.com)

Cooper Mountain (O/B): Oregon (www.coopermountainwine.com)

Fitzpatrick Winery (O): California (www.fitzpatrickwinery.com)

Four Chimneys (O): New York (www.fourchimneysorganicwine.com)

Frey (O/B): California; a longtime GreenerPenny fave (www.freywine.com)

Larocca Vineyards (O): California (www.laroccavineyards.com)

Ponzi Wines (LIVE/Salmon Safe): Oregon (www.ponziwines.com)

Resonance Vineyard (B): Oregon (www.resonancevineyard.com)

Sokol Blosser Vineyards (O/Salmon Safe): Oregon (www.sokolblosser.com)

To find more good green wines, check out these sites, and ask at your local farmers' market and wine shops.

Appellation Wines (www.appellationnyc.com)

Natural Merchants (www.naturalmerchants.com)

Organic Vintners (www.organicvintners.com)

The Organic Wine Company (www.theorganicwinecompany.com)

Organic Wine Press: Bargain prices for excellent domestic and imported organic wines (www.organicwinepress.com)

EUROPEAN PICKS

Asthmatics often prefer white wines, which, as a rule, contain far lower quantities of sulfites. Among the best I've recently tried:

Bodegas Iranzo: Europe's oldest organic wine; dry and sparkling, from Spanish vineyards founded in 1335 (www.naturalmerchants.com)

Cantina Pizzolato Pino Grigio: golden, fruity; from a family vineyard in Treviso, Italy (www.organicwinepress.com)

FAIR TRADE WINE

It hasn't quite caught on in the United States yet, but fair trade wine is big in Europe. Here, three sources:

Etica certified fair trade wines from Argentina, Chile, and South Africa: available by mail order only (www.eticawine.com);

Malbec's Neu Direction certified Fair Trade wine from Argentina: available through Walmart's Sam's Club, or at www.organicwinetradecompany.com; and

Melania certified fair trade wines from Chile: available in some U.S. stores or at www.melaniawines.com.

LOCAL WINE

Ask for it at your local wine store, and sign up for regional wine tastings. Also see www.localwineevents.com.

For more information, log on to www.greenerpenny.com.

Beer

Why organic beer? It's better for the environment and thus our overall health, from the growing of the barley and hops without petrochemical pesticides and fertilizers, to the strict limitation on chemicals used in brewing and even cleaning the factory equipment. In order to sport the USDA Organic seal, a beer must have at least 95 percent organic ingredients.

Here are some organic brews, at least one of which you can probably find at a local supermarket, or at Whole Foods or Wild Oats.

Butte Creek (www.buttecreek.com)

Eel River (www.eelriverbrewing.com)

Peak Organic (www.peakbrewing.com)

Stone Mill Pale Ale (Anheuser-Busch) (www.stonemillpaleale.com)

Wolaver's (www.ottercreekbrewing.com)

The best quick and easy way to find local beer is to search for a brewpub or microbrewery at www.beer100.com. You may be pleasantly surprised at all your options. For example, every Hawaiian island has at least one locally made brew, an especially hopeful trend in a state that imports more than 80 percent of its food. Another online microbrewery source: www.brewpubzone.

> For more info on microbreweries and tips on making your own, see
> **www.beeradvocate.com.**

Organic food may give nutrition a boost.

A HOPS LOOPHOLE

Brewers are permitted to use non-organic hops if they can't get "sufficient quantities" of organic. If you want to taste a truly 95 percent organic brew, ask companies if they use organic hops, and seek out regional organic microbreweries, which don't require the quantities of hops that big national companies do. Some biggies, though, such as Wolaver's (see list to left) ensure that they use organic hops in their organic beers.

By choosing fish that are
plentiful enough to keep reproducing
in the wild, consumers direct
marketplace change.

ONE GREEN THING

Eat small fry like sardines, rather than big hunks, like bluefin tuna.

Why? They're healthier for the seas. Smaller fish, in general, reproduce quickly and thus are more abundant and not overfished. Large predators such as bluefin tuna mature late, so you risk eating juveniles before they have a chance to reproduce, and mamma fish at the peak of their fertility.

They're also healthier for you. Smaller fish eat low on the food chain, are shorter-lived, and thus collect fewer toxins in their fat than do big, long-lived predators such as swordfish. Sardines, for example, are very high in omega-3 fatty acids (2.7 grams per 100 grams) and are very low in mercury compared with most other fish.

REELING IN THE FACTS

Perhaps no food serves up as much confusion as fish. On the one hand, fish are healthful, full of heart- and brain-protecting omega-3 fats. On the other hand, they can be unhealthful, polluted with brain-damaging mercury or PCBs (polychlorinated biphenyls). And many species are so overfished they're in danger of disappearing altogether!

Here's how many sardines you'd have to eat to get the same amount of mercury exposure you get with canned tuna and swordfish:

One can of chunk light tuna = 6 sardines

One 6-ounce serving of swordfish = 48.5 sardines

most-asked question

Which fish are safest to eat for humans and the seas?

In general, smaller, younger, vegetarian fish are best for both. (For details, see the "Choose It/Lose It" table on pages 38–39.) However, because you can't always find fish that are best for both your health and the seas, I have provided two additional lists that allow you to make the best choice depending on your scenario. If you are in a situation where health is your top concern, there is a separate "Choose It/Lose It" table for this (see page 41). Similarly, if the environment is your top priority, refer to the third "Choose It/Lose It" table (see page 47). In this manner, you will always be armed with the best knowledge. Take note that some fish appear in more than one table and that where a fish comes from can make a world of difference—Pacific populations are frequently less depleted than those in the Atlantic.

BEST FOR YOU AND THE SEA*

choose it

The following seafood comes from healthy populations that are well managed and not overfished or farmed destructively. They are also not high in mercury or PCBs.

Arctic char (F)

Barramundi (F)

Bass, striped (F)

Catfish, U.S. (F)

Clams

Cod, Pacific and Alaska

Crab: Dungeness, Stone, King (Alaska), snow (imitation/surimi)

Flounder and sole, Pacific (true varieties, including English sole—plus sanddabs)

Haddock (hook-and-line caught)

Halibut, Pacific

Herring (Atlantic sardines)

Lobster, U.S./Maine

Mackerel, (Atlantic)

Mussels (F)

Oysters, wild (F)

Perch, Great Lakes, Alaska, B.C.

Pollock, Wild Alaska (fish sticks)

Sablefish/Black cod, also known as butterfish

Salmon, wild Alaskan (fresh or canned); wild Washington

Sardines, Pacific

Scallops, bay (F)

Scallops, sea (W)

Shrimp, U.S. (F or W)

Smelt, U.S.

Snapper, red, wild Alaskan, B.C.

Squid

Tilapia, U.S. (F)

Trout, rainbow (F)

Tuna, albacore (white, tombo), U.S., Canada (troll or pole-caught)

Skipjack tuna (troll/pole, fresh or canned) (chunk light)

Yellowtail, skipjack tuna, U.S. (Kona Kampachi) (F)

*F = farmed; W = wild-caught

The following seafood is endangered, farmed in destructive ways, and/or is high in mercury, PCBs, or dioxins.

Bass, striped (W)

Chilean sea bass (Patagonian Toothfish)

Cod, Atlantic

Crab, blue

Flounder and sole, Atlantic including related varieties: winter flounder, lemon sole, sanddabs, fluke, and plaice

Grouper

Haddock, trawl-caught

Halibut, Atlantic

Mackerel (King)

Marlin, blue

Marlin, striped

Monkfish

Octopus

Orange Roughy

Pike

Salmon (including "Atlantic") (F)

Shark

Shrimp, imported

Snapper, pink, Pacific (except NW Hawaiian)

Snapper, red, Pacific (except NW Hawaiian)

Swordfish

Tilapia, Asia (F)

Tilefish (also known as Golden Snapper)

Tuna, albacore (white, tombo), (fresh or canned), Imported, long-line

Tuna, bluefin (Toro)

Tuna, bigeye, yellowfin, long-line

Yellowtail, Australia or Japan (F)

If health is your primary concern, the following "Choose It" column is divided into four groups of fish, ranging from those lowest in mercury and PCBs; these can be eaten once a week, or four times a month plus a little more. Those that are moderately high in these contaminants shouldn't be eaten more than once a month.

Children, who are smaller and still developing, should eat fish less frequently than adults do, as a general rule.

The "Lose It" column lists the highest-mercury fish, which everyone had best avoid. It's a lot shorter than the list of fish you can safely eat!

How many fish meals does that make? It depends on which group the fish comes from, and on balancing your intake over time. For instance, you can safely eat up to four 6-ounce servings of the lowest-mercury fish per month. If you eat a moderate-mercury fish that's allowed twice a month, that's the equivalent of four lowest-mercury fish servings. Don't worry about being absolutely precise with your math. My ratings have an extra margin of caution built in.

Note that some fish, such as true flounder and sole, can safely be eaten four times a month regardless of where they're caught; but for other species, the source still matters: for instance, albacore tuna (tombo ahi) from the U.S. and Canada is safer to eat than albacore from abroad.

Smaller fish, in general, are more abundant and not overfished.

BEST FISH FOR YOUR HEALTH

👍 choose it

Best of the Best: The following fish are lowest in mercury and PCBs. It's safe for women to eat a 6-ounce serving of fish from this group slightly more than once a week, or 4-plus times a month.*

Anchovies

Catfish, U.S. (F)**

Clams

Crab: Dungeness, Stone, King, snow (imitation/surimi)

Crawfish

Flounder and sole, true varieties, including English sole—plus sanddabs, plaice

Haddock

Herring (Atlantic sardines)

Mackerel, Atlantic

Mussels (F)

Oysters (F)

Pollock, Wild Alaska (fish sticks)

Salmon, Alaska (fresh or canned) (W)

Sardines

👎 lose it

The following fish are high in mercury or PCBs, both of which can cause nervous system damage and learning problems, and should not be eaten at all. Imported farmed shrimp are on this list because they may contain antibiotics that are banned from use in the United States.

Alewife

Bass, striped (W)

Bluefish

Croaker, white

Eel, regular

Mackerel (King)

Marlin

Shad

Shark

Shrimp, imported

Sturgeon, imported (W)

Swordfish

Tuna, albacore (tombo), Imported

Tuna, bluefin

Weakfish

*For more specific allowances according to age and sex, see www.edf.org/seafood.
**F = farmed; W = wild-caught

Scallops

Shrimp, U.S. or Canadian

Squid

Tilapia, U.S/Latin America (F)

Tuna, albacore (tombo, U.S/Canada only

The following contain moderately low levels of mercury or PCBs; from this group, up to four 6-ounce servings a month can safely be eaten by adults.

Arctic char (F)	Oysters (W)
Barramundi (F)	Pompano, U.S.
Bass, black sea	Porgy, red, U.S.
Bass, striped (F)	Sablefish/black cod/butterfish
Cod	Skate
Halibut	Snapper (all types except mutton)
Lobster, spiny, U.S./Australia/Baja	Sole
Mahimahi, U.S	Trout, rainbow (F)
Monkfish	Yellowtail, F (Hamachi, Kampachi)

These fish contain moderate levels of mercury or PCBs and can be eaten two to three times a month by adults.

Albacore tuna (canned white)	Lingcod
Crab, blue	Mackerel, Spanish
Eel, conger	Oysters (W)
Grouper	Perch, Great Lakes

Rockfish

Smelt, U.S.

Snapper, mutton

Sturgeon, Atlantic

Tilefish (Golden Snapper)

Tuna, yellowfin

Wahoo

Last, to Eat the Least: The following fish are higher in mercury or PCBs, and should be limited to once a month.

Croaker, Atlantic

Flounder and sole, related varieties: summer and winter flounder/fluke/plaice

Opah (moonfish)

Salmon (Atlantic) (F)

Salmon (Washington) (W)

Tuna, Bigeye

better for your health

The high protein, omega fatty acids, and low saturated fats in fish are great for your body and your brain—and your baby's, if you're pregnant or planning to be. You can reap the full benefits, however, only if you avoid fish containing high levels of mercury and man-made chemicals known as polychlorinated biphenyls (PCBs), both of which attack the brain and nervous system, cross the placenta from mother to fetus, and can cause developmental delays and lower IQs in children. Mercury is far more common in fish; PCBs tend to be found in fish from freshwater bodies, such as the Hudson River, where the chemicals now banned in the U.S., were discharged by industry. Another man-made contaminant, dioxin, is found in higher levels in farmed salmon than in wild. In high doses, dioxins have been found to cause cancer and infertility.

Mercury overexposure in adults can produce memory problems, hair loss, and fatigue, and can contribute to cardiovascular disease. While mercury is flushed from the body over time, alleviating symptoms of poisoning in adults, permanent harm can be done to fetuses and young children, who are so much smaller and whose bodies and brains are rapidly developing.

> *Because it can take up to a year for adults to return to safe mercury blood levels, women who may become pregnant should minimize the amount they're exposed to in fish—while still reaping health benefits by eating low-mercury fish.*

GOOD NEWS!

Mercury blood levels in American women declined from 1999 to 2004, the most recent date for which statistics are available. The reason? Women are still eating the same amount of fish, so they must be choosing to eat lower-mercury species!

And there's more good news: The benefits of eating fish certainly exceed the risks, if one chooses low-mercury varieties.

THE BOTTOM LINE: HOW MUCH FISH CAN YOU SAFELY EAT?

Fish and shellfish are good for your health, and eating a variety of different fish, rather than what's popular at the moment, will do a lot to even out the risks for both you and the environment. "If you regularly eat seafood that's low in mercury or PCBs, the odd piece that's high in contaminants probably won't do you harm," says Timothy Fitzgerald, oceans scientist with the Environmental Defense Fund (EDF).

Women

Women who are nursing, pregnant, or planning to be, should eat no more than 12 ounces (or two meals) per week of lower-mercury fish, a joint advisory by the EPA and FDA recommended in 2004. (See www.cfsan.fda.gov.) FDA guidelines assume a 6-ounce serving of fish per meal.

Children

Children younger than five should eat a little less than one 6-ounce serving of the lowest-mercury fish a week, says the Environmental Working Group, which has a helpful tuna calculator on its website. To find your safe limit, enter your weight and sex in their tuna calculator. (Go to www.ewg.org/tunacalculator.)

DROP IT!

Please don't eat these two species:

1. **Although Chilean sea bass is a moderate-mercury fish that can be safely eaten twice a month, according to the EDF, it is egregiously overfished, so please give it a pass, as conservation groups and enlightened chefs have been urging for years. It was renamed for marketing purposes and isn't actually a bass at all. Its real name is the Patagonian toothfish.**

2. **Orange roughy is higher in mercury, but can still be eaten once a month, per the EDF. I'd still skip it, even if it's the only fish on the menu, because these long-lived and mysterious South Pacific creatures are in danger of extinction. Besides, when you think about it, who wants to eat anything that's been around for eighty years?**

If you are more concerned with the impact of your fish choice on the environment, the "Choose It/Lose It" table, at right, takes into account only the environmental impact of a given fish, without regard to contaminants. The "Choose It" section is divided into two parts: "Ocean's Best" and "Second Best." The "Lose It" section consists of the "Ocean's Worst" fish, whose production, whether wild-caught or farmed, causes the most environmental harm.

BEST FOR THE SEAS

👍 *choose it*   👎 *lose it*

OCEAN'S BEST

The following seafood comes from healthy populations that are well managed and fished or farmed in environmentally sounder ways.

- Anchovies
- Arctic char (F)
- Barramundi, U.S. (F)
- Bass, striped (F or W)
- Catfish, U.S. (F)
- Clams
- Cod, Pacific (Alaska)
- Crab: Dungeness, Stone
- Halibut, Pacific
- Lobster, spiny, U.S.
- Mackerel, Atlantic
- Mullet
- Mussels (F)
- Octopus, Hawaii/California (W)
- Oysters (F)
- Pollock, Alaska (fish sticks)
- Salmon, Alaska (fresh or canned) (W)
- Scallops, bay (F)

OCEAN'S WORST

The following seafood is endangered or overfished, or being harvested or farmed in destructive ways.

- Chilean sea bass (Patagonian toothfish)
- Cod, Atlantic
- Flounder and sole, Atlantic
- Grouper
- Haddock, trawl
- Halibut, Atlantic
- Mackerel (King)
- Mahimahi, imported
- Marlin
- Monkfish
- Octopus (except Hawaii/California)
- Orange roughy
- Rockfish, Pacific (trawled)
- Salmon (including "Atlantic") (F)
- Shark
- Shrimp, imported
- Snapper, red
- Sole, Atlantic

Sturgeon and caviar, F

Tuna, albacore, U.S., British Columbia (troll/pole caught)

SECOND BEST

The following fish are currently under more fishing pressure, and should not be consumed regularly.

Cod, Pacific (trawled)

Crab, Blue, King (Alaska), snow (imitation/surimi)

Flounder, Pacific

Herring (Atlantic sardines)

Lobster, U.S., Maine

Mahimahi, U.S.

Oysters (W)

Scallops, sea

Shrimp, U.S. (F or W)

Sole, Pacific

Squid

Swordfish, U.S.

Tuna, bigeye (troll/pole)

Tuna, Skipjack (troll, pole) (fresh or canned) (chunk light)

Tuna, yellowfin (troll/pole)

Sturgeon and caviar, imported (W)

Swordfish, imported

Tilefish (also known as Golden Snapper)

Tuna, albacore, imported (long-line caught) (fresh or canned)

Tuna, bigeye (long-line)

Tuna, bluefin (Toro, Maguro)

Tuna, yellowfin (long-line)

Yellowtail, Australia or Japan (F)

Safety Swap: Replace one 6-ounce can of albacore "white" tuna with one 6-ounce can of wild Alaska salmon, and reduce your mercury intake by 89 percent.

Source: I am indebted to EDF's Eco-best fish list (www.edf.org) and the Monterey Bay Aquarium's Seafood Selector (www.mbayaq.org) for this list.

better for the planet

 When we avoid eating overfished and destructively farmed species, we help ocean ecosystems recover. By choosing fish that are plentiful enough to keep reproducing in the wild, or farmed in fully contained land-based systems, consumers direct marketplace change away from the following detrimental practices:

Overfishing

Seventy-five percent of worldwide fisheries are on the verge of collapse due to pollution, habitat reduction, and overfishing, according to the United Nations Food and Agriculture Organization. Since 1960, there's been a 90 percent reduction in populations of large wild predator fish, the "tigers of the sea," including tuna, cod, swordfish, and halibut. Destructive fishing methods, such as bottom trawls and long lines, destroy the ocean floor and kill untargeted species, such as endangered sea turtles, birds, and mammals, as "bycatch."

How Was This Fish Caught?

Wild-capture fisheries are the most damaging businesses taking place in the ocean right now. For example, 18–40 million tons of "bycatch," i.e., fish and marine mammals caught unintentionally, which comprise as much as half of the official harvest—are killed and discarded every year. To counter this and allow fish populations to recover, fishermen and conservationists are working together to set catch limits and adopt more sustainable fishing practices.

SAFE VERSUS HARMFUL FISHING METHODS

👍 choose it

Choose fish certified as taken sustainably by well-managed fisheries by the Marine Stewardship Council (www.MSC.org).

Choose fish bearing the label of Ecofish (www.ecofish.com), administered by an alliance of conservation-minded fishermen and environmental scientists.

Ask at the fish counter for seafood that is taken under the auspices of Limited Access Privilege Programs (LAPPs) and Community Supported Fisheries (CSFs). These programs aim to protect fishermen's livelihoods by ensuring them catch shares, at the same time restricting the number of fish taken and requiring less destructive fishing methods.

Ask for fish caught using the following gentler methods:

> Scottish, or net trawls, which do not scrape the bottom but are suspended above it by a network of rollers and pulleys;

> Troll, pole, and hook-and-line, which require close monitoring and oversight by fishermen, permitting catch limits and release of bycatch; and

> Nets with turtle-exclusion devices (TEDs), now used by most domestic U.S. shrimpers.

For more information on LAPPs and greener fishing methods, see www.edf.org.

👎 lose it

Avoid fish and shellfish caught with these industrial-scale methods, all of which kill substantial bycatch:

> Conventional trawls, which are dragged across the ocean bottom, destroying reefs and other habitats;

> Drift and seine nets, which cover vast areas and entangle and smother marine mammals, birds, and turtles; and

> Long lines, which overharvest big breeding fish in the open ocean.

Industrial Fish Farming

Because farmed carnivorous fish, such as salmon, are fed a diet of fish meal with concentrated protein that includes small wild forage fish (e.g., anchovies), they are in competition with wild fish (and humans) for food.

Fish farmed in offshore net pens foul waters with their nitrogen-heavy wastes, contributing to oxygen-depleted coastal dead zones, which have doubled in size every ten years since 1960, to a total 147,000 square miles—an area as big as New Zealand—in 2008. Disease outbreaks among closely packed farmed fish can threaten wild populations.

Mangrove forests and other ocean habitat are destroyed to create shrimp farms.

CANNED FISH

choose it

Choose canned wild Alaska salmon, which is certified sustainable by the Marine Stewardship Council (MSC). At less than $3 per 7-ounce can, it's one third to half the price per pound of fresh. Great value for your budget and the environment.

lose it

Lose the canned albacore tuna lacking the "U.S. troll or hand-line caught" and/or MSC seal awarded to protective fishing methods. It's high in mercury and costly to the environment.

LOCAL SAFETY NETS

Before eating locally caught fresh or saltwater fish and shellfish, especially after a heavy rain, check health department advisories.

Why? These fish may contain higher levels of toxic chemicals or bacteria from local sewage or oil/industrial spills.

For levels of PCBs, DDT, and chlordane (a nasty pesticide), check the EPA's list of local advisories at www.epa.gov/waterscience/fish/. Search by state to find a map of the affected bodies of water (lakes, rivers, bays).

To check on mercury advisories in your state, see EWG's database at
www.ewg.org/node/8151.

FISH CARDS PROVIDE NET ECO GAINS

The Fish List combines the expertise of the Blue Ocean Institute, the Environmental Defense Fund, and the Monterey Bay Aquarium. See www.thefishlist.org/. The Monterey Bay Aquarium's fish cards, at www.mbayaq.org listing "eco-best," "good alternative," and "avoid" choices for every region of the country, are a totally awesome tool, and are updated every six months, to boot. And EDF's user-friendly Seafood Selector tool can be found at www.edf.org. You can call Blue Ocean's cool Fish Phone from your cell (1-877-BOI-SEAS) or visit www.blueocean.org/seafood/seafood-guide. Each of the groups also has its own sushi guide, including the Japanese names for the fish.

Children, who are smaller and still developing, should eat fish less frequently than adults do, as a general rule.

If all Americans skipped meat for one day a week, it would reduce . . . carbon emissions as much as taking 20 million midsize cars off the road for one year.

4

Meat, Dairy, Poultry, and Eggs

ONE GREEN THING

Skip red meat at least one day a week.

Why? You'll probably live longer. A 2009 study of more than half a million American men and women found that those who ate more red meat were likely to die sooner of heart disease and cancer than those who ate less red meat.

Why else? Climate-wise, eating less meat is one of the biggest little steps you can take. Skip red meat for just one day, and you'll reduce the same amount of greenhouse gas emissions as driving 760 fewer miles a year. If all Americans skipped meat for one day (i.e., three meals) a week, it would reduce the equivalent in carbon emissions as much as taking 20 million midsize cars off the road for one year.

And you don't have to go cold turkey! Just replace the meat with a serving of poultry, eggs, or fish.

Skip a hamburger, and save the more than 10,000 liters of water required to produce it.

MEAT

better for your health

Eating More Vegetables and Fewer Animal Foods

Vegetarians and "healthy eaters" who consume small amounts of meat and fish live longer, according to a twenty-five-year study by the German Cancer Research Center released in 2005. Among the nearly two thousand vegetarians in the study, men had a 50 percent reduced risk of early death, and 30 percent of women lived longer, compared with the general population.

> People who eat eight servings of fruit and vegetables per day are 30 percent less likely to have a heart attack or stroke than those who eat only 1.5 servings, according to the Harvard Nurses' Health Study.

better for the planet

Meat production causes more environmental harm—including the release of greenhouse gas, spillage of animal wastes into waterways, use of water and pesticides to grow feed crops for animals, and deforestation caused by farms and ranches—than that of any other food, according to the Union of Concerned Scientists (UCS). Livestock production is responsible for 18 percent of GHG emissions worldwide, and on average, red meat and dairy is around 150 percent more GHG-intensive than chicken or fish.

Why? It's what the livestock emit. From their digestive tracts, ungulate (hoofed) animals—including cows, pigs, sheep, and goats—burp and otherwise release gaseous methane, a GHG that's twenty-three times more potent than CO_2! That's why the head of the UN's International Panel on Climate Change (IPCC) has asked us all to eat less meat.

Meat production also wastes water. It takes 7 to 10 pounds of grain and 43,000 liters of water to produce 1 pound of beef. Compare this with the 1,000 liters of water needed to produce a pound of grain. Skip a hamburger, and save the more than 10,000 liters of water required to produce it.

better for your budget

 Meat generally costs more per pound than vegetable protein sources such as beans and tofu, the Union of Concerned Scientists says. Sources of protein such as tofu and beans are generally 30 to 40 percent cheaper than animal products.

CALCULATE THE CARBON IN YOUR DIET

Get instant, fun feedback on the GHG you'll expend with every meal with *Bon Appetit*'s Low Carbon Diet Calculator. On the website, you are presented with a cast-iron fry pan and photos of various menu options for breakfast, lunch, or dinner. Click on and drag your selection into the pan, and its carbon points appear. A high-carbon diet is 4,500 points a day; a cheeseburger and fries are 2,000 points, and grilled local vegetables in season, a mere 95. See www.eatlowcarbon.org.

most-asked question

I get confused by all the different "green" claims on meat, poultry, and eggs. Which labels ensure me the best choice for my money?

Choose animal products bearing the green claims in the "Choose It" column of the following table.

TRUSTED LABELS FOR MEAT, POULTRY, AND EGGS

choose it

Look for the following, third-party-verified labels on poultry, eggs, dairy, and meat. Antibiotics are given only to sick animals; no growth hormones; no feeding of animal parts to animals, a process that has been implicated in bovine spongiform encephalitis, or "mad cow" disease.

BEST PICKS

AMERICAN GRASSFED ASSOCIATION: Cows, sheep, and goats eat grass, period, and this standard requires that they spend most of their lives outside, in a pasture. Third-party-certified by the Food Alliance (see later in this list). Sick animals, if given antibiotics,

lose it

Don't be taken in by these labels:

ANIMAL CARE CERTIFIED/UNITED EGG PRODUCER: There is no third-party verification of humane treatment of creatures.

ANTIBIOTIC FREE/RAISED WITHOUT ANTIBIOTICS/NO ANTIBIOTICS ADMINISTERED: While permitted as a label by USDA, it is considered meaningless by the Consumers Union; it is verified only by the companies themselves, rather than a third party.

FREE RANGE OR FREE ROAMING: There is no guarantee that the cows, chickens, or anyone else actually got outdoors.

FRESH (ON POULTRY): It could actually have once been frozen.

Meat, Dairy, Poultry, and Eggs

continued on p. 60 59

are removed from the program. (See www.ameri-cangrassfed.org.)

ANIMAL WELFARE APPROVED: This family farm label guarantees that cows and chickens spend most of their lives in the fields; has very specific humane handling and shelter standards; and gets top ratings from the World Society for Protection of Animals. (See www.animalwelfareapproved.org.)

CERTIFIED HUMANE: Pasture time is not speci-fied, although humane shelter (enough space to freely move about; no crates, cages, or being tied in stalls) and handling are. (See www.certifiedhu mane.org.)

DEMETER biodynamic (meat, milk, cheese, eggs): Animals are guaranteed exercise and humane treatment. (See www.demeter.net, www.demeter usa.org.)

FOOD ALLIANCE CERTIFIED: Sets clear standards for lifetime access to pasture and humane treat-ment, including slaughtering. (See www.foodal-liance.org.)

"GRASS FED": The USDA de-fines this as the animal ate only 100 percent grass in its life, but third-party verifica-tion is not required.

USDA "NATURALLY RAISED": These products contain no hormones* or artificial color-ings, and only a few antibi-otics are allowed, but there's no third-party verification.

USDA PROCESS VERIFIED CERTIFIED GRASS (Forage) FED: Animals' access to pas-ture is required, but not guaranteed; they can be fed on hay in stalls and still qualify for the label. Antibi-otics and growth hormones are permitted. (See www.usda.gov for more in-formation.)

USDA ORGANIC: Better for you, but not necessarily for the animals. They eat only 100 percent certified organic grass, corn, or grain, and sick animals given antibiotics are removed from the program, but while they're required to have "access" to pasture, this is not clearly defined. (See www.ams/usda.gov/nop.)

MAINE QUALITY TRADEMARK (MILK): No growth hormones are used; animal welfare is respected. (See www.state.me.us/agriculture /qar/qtrad mark.html.)

*In conventional animal farming, growth hormones are routinely given to cattle and chickens, but not to pigs.

better for your health

Avoiding antibiotics in food is important if you don't want antibiotic-resistant bacteria growing in your system. Seventy percent of antibiotics produced in the United States are fed to livestock.

Grass-fed beef has fewer saturated fats and higher levels of heart-healthy omega-3 fats, according to the Union of Concerned Scientists.

better for the planet

If you eat less meat, you'll conserve water and greenhouse gases. Fifty percent of the corn grown in the United States goes toward feeding livestock. In addition to methane, beef's carbon footprint includes the heat-trapping nitrous oxide emitted by synthetic fertilizers used to grow feed grains. Pasture raised, or grass-fed, beef is climate-cooler because grasses require less fertilizer and pesticide (if any at all) than grain, according to the Union of Concerned Scientists.

For more information, see the Union of Concerned Scientists website, **www.ucusa.org.**

Livestock production is responsible for 18 percent of greenhouse gas (GHG) emissions worldwide.

To cut back on saturated fats, my husband and I resolved to eat at least two meatless, cheeseless dinners a week. The first thing we noticed was that we were really savoring and enjoying the true taste of vegetables in main dishes such as vegetarian chili with carrots and celery, bok choy and red pepper stir fried over brown rice, and whole-wheat pasta with mushrooms, kale, and peas—all with plenty of onions and garlic. The second discovery was that my husband liked tofu if it was mixed into a spicy dish.

VEGETARIANS WITH A CONSCIENCE

To ensure that your veggie's green standards are met, choose eggs and dairy bearing these labels:

- Animal Welfare Approved (www.animalwelfareapproved.org)
- Certified Humane Raised & Handled (www.certifiedhumane.com)
- Food Alliance Certified (www.foodalliance.org)

To find grass-fed, local animal products, go to www.eatwild.org and click on the map for "grass-fed."

CAN A VEGETARIAN DIET PROVIDE ENOUGH PROTEIN AND CALCIUM?

Yes.

Vegetable protein sources: peas and beans, nuts, soy products (tofu, tempeh, veggie burgers, soy yogurt, and soy cheese)

Calcium: dark leafy greens, soy products, calcium-fortified orange juice, and breakfast cereals

For more information and how-tos on nutritionally complete vegetarian diets, including sources of those all-important B vitamins, go to www.mypyramid.gov/tips_resources/vegetarian_diets.html.

DAIRY

Having agreed to make room in our budget for organic versions of the fruits and vegetables our child ate most, my husband and I had another "aha!" moment when we learned that genetically engineered recombinant bovine growth hormone, or rBGH, is routinely given to conventional dairy cows to make them produce more milk. Actually, it makes them overproduce. Not only is this painful to the cows, whose udders become unnaturally swollen and more prone to infection, but it also poses unnecessary risks to human health.

Why? Infections lead to the cows' being treated more frequently with antibiotics This increases the likelihood that antibiotic-resistant bacteria will develop in the bodies of those who drink their milk. And milk from rBGH-treated cows contains residues of an insulin-growth-promoting hormone that's suspected of playing a role in diabetes and breast cancer.

The solution? Easy. Organic milk is guaranteed free of antibiotics and hormones. Many non-organic dairies have foresworn the use of rBGH, and their milk is priced competitively with the conventional variety. Thanks to consumer demand, big companies such as Dannon, General Mills, and Wal-Mart are taking action to ban rBGH from the dairy foods they sell.

Check out this list to find rBGH-free milk in your locale:
www.organicconsumers.org/rBGH/rbghlist.cfm

Meat, Dairy, Poultry, and Eggs

63

Choosing glass is best for the planet and your health; it's infinitely recyclable and does not leach any chemicals.

Food Storage and Cookware

5

ONE GREEN THING

Never microwave food in plastics. Use tempered glass or ceramic instead.

Why? Tests show that even "microwave safe" plastic containers release a toxic chemical known as Bisphenol A (BPA) into their contents when heated normally.

TOXIC PLASTIC CHEMICALS

Bisphenol A

This chemical, widely used in polycarbonate plastics, has been linked to developmental harm in lab animals, and, recently, to heart disease, diabetes, and liver cancer in humans. The National Toxicology Program has warned that BPA may interfere with normal development in human infants. BPA can be released when plastic is heated, damaged, or worn.

Phthalates

These plasticizing chemicals are also found to be disruptive to male reproductive development and virility. They have also been implicated in childhood asthma. Phthalates migrate readily out of PVC plastics and synthetic fragrances.

What about plastic containers for storing food in the fridge or at room temperature? Do they contain BPA, too?

Some do, some don't. Not all plastics are created alike; they can usually be identified by recycling codes, see the "Choose It/Lose It" table below. (For the "Plastics by the Numbers," see page 10.)

SAFE PLASTIC

👍 *choose it*

Safest plastic food containers are made of:

- Low-density polyethylene (LDPE), with the recycling code #4 in the "chasing arrows" triangle

- Polypropylene (PP), code #5

These two plastics have not been shown to leach toxic BPA or other chemicals when unheated. However, if heated, any plastic may leach.

👎 *lose it*

Avoid containers made of:

- Polycarbonate plastic (PC), with the recycling code #7 in the "chasing arrows" triangle. PC containers can release toxic BPA, heated or not.

- Polystyrene (PS), code #6, which can leach styrene, a possible human carcinogen. It's commonly used in white Styrofoam takeout clamshells and coffee cups, and in clear clamshells and disposable utensils.

Food Storage and Cookware

another question

What's the safest plastic wrap?

Choose by the numbers. Yes to #4, but no to #3.

SAFE FOOD WRAP

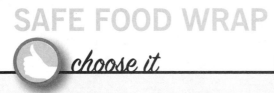

choose it   lose it

Buy food wraps made of these safer, greener materials:

- Low-density polyethylene (LDPE), which bears the recycling code #4 (in the "arrow" triangle). Brands include Best Yet, Glad, and Saran Cling Wrap.

- Green (unbleached) and/or vegetable wax and parchment papers, available at www.greenfeet.com and Whole Foods supermarkets.

Avoid wraps made of:

- Polyvinyl chloride, or vinyl (PVC #3)

Toxic, unstable chemicals known as phthalates, used to make plastics flexible, readily leach out of soft PVC.

Most deli cheeses and meats come in PVC (#3), but at home you can re-wrap them in safer plastics or papers.

The safer plastics for our health

are also safer for the planet!

better for your health

Keeping food out of contact with plastics containing BPA and phthalates is one simple, painless way to reduce exposure to these man-made chemicals, which have been found in more than 90 percent of Americans in "body burden" studies by the U.S. Centers for Disease Control. In scientific studies, phthalates and BPA have shown the ability to interrupt normal nervous and reproductive system development in lab animals and, in recent years, in humans. Both chemicals imitate the female hormone estrogen and suppress the male hormone testosterone, and have been linked to obesity and diabetes in humans.

Phthalates are used in synthetic fragrances as well as in PVC plastic. For more on the health and environmental impact of phthalates, turn to the section on "Perfume" in chapter 11.

better for the planet

The safer plastics for our health are also safer for the planet! For one thing, they're recyclable. Items made of LDPE #4, the plastic used in shopping bags, are accepted at many plastic-bag recycling centers, and at many local grocery and big-box stores. PP #5 is accepted by most municipal curbside recycling programs. But PVC #3 and PC #7 are generally not recyclable. By not buying vinyl or polycarbonate wraps and containers, we keep them out of landfills, and prevent them from releasing their toxic chemicals into soil and water.

Choosing glass is best for the planet and your health because it's infinitely recyclable and does not leach any chemicals.

another question

What if I don't see a plastic recycling code on a container?

Check the item by brand and name against my regularly updated Safe Plastic Food Storage Containers, which includes selected Gladware, Rubbermaid, and Tupperware items, at www.greenerpenny.com You can also access GreenerPenny shopping lists and tips on your cell phone. If it's not on my list, or unbranded, remember this mantra: When in doubt, don't buy!

"NON-MICROWAVE SAFE" IS MORE LIKE IT!

In 2008, lab tests found BPA in microwaved food containers and heated plastic-lined cans. What was most startling: Even non-polycarbonate (#7) plastics stamped with the recycling numbers 1, 2, and 5 leached BPA when heated. The moral of the story? Don't microwave plastic!

The safest plastic food containers are made of low-density polyethylene (LDPE), or polypropylene (PP).

On my first day as editor of *The Green Guide* in 1996, I asked my coworker why she transferred her premade vegetarian meal from its plastic container to a ceramic bowl before heating it in the microwave oven. "The manufacturers say it's safe to zap it in the plastic, but I don't. The plastic leaches into the food," Mary Lou said. It was the first time I'd ever heard about leaching, but I gathered from her grim tone that it was pretty undesirable! I'll always be grateful to Mary Lou for introducing me to this problem, and for demonstrating a simple daily solution.

MICROWAVE-SAFE FOOD CONTAINERS

Tempered glass containers are made by Anchor Hocking, Frigoverre, and Pyrex. I also recommend ceramic CorningWare with glass lids.

THE OTHER, BPA-FREE #7 PLASTICS

It's kind of complicated, but that's life: bad PC (#7) plastic has two good—well, so far, so good—new siblings that have not been found to leach BPA, phthalates, or other toxic chemicals.

Bioplastics (PLA)

The latest green thing in food service and takeout ware are "compostable" bioplastic clamshells, plates, and bowls made of polylactide (PLA) resin derived from corn or potatoes, or bagasse, made from sugarcane waste.

Because they are made from renewable vegetable resources, bioplastics are preferable to regular, petroleum-derived plastics. Plus, they require 25 to 55 percent less fossil fuels to produce than does plastic made from petroleum. Many

Food Storage and Cookware

71

are washable, and hence reusable (although not yet as durable as some regular plastics).

The drawbacks: Like all #7 plastics, bioplastics are not easily recyclable. Nor are they easily compostable, unless you're an institution. That's because in order to properly biodegrade within three months (as opposed to years), bioplastics must be treated at high temperatures in industrial composters. If dumped in landfills, they will take years to biodegrade, if at all; and when they do decompose, they release methane, a major greenhouse gas.

Your best option is probably to check with supermarkets or restaurants/delis that use bioplastics and ask them to take back your cleaned containers. You can suggest that they take the bioplastics to an industrial composter in the area. Perhaps they can team up with other stores and restaurants to do so.

GreenerPenny's Tips

BIOPLASTIC

Put bioplastics in the correct recycling bin! If you're eating in a cafeteria or takeout restaurant that uses bioplastic serving ware, put your used items in the bin labeled for plates, cups, and utensils—not in the trash or paper or bottle/can recycling bins.

Is bioplastic certified compostable? Before you buy, look for the Biodegradable Products Institute/USA Composting Council "Compostable" label, BPI/USA, which certifies that the item will biodegrade in an industrial composter.

Some certified compostable bioplastic products include trash, kitchen, yard, and pet-waste bags (www.biobagusa.com or reusablebags.com), and unbleached bagasse plates and bowls (www.greenhome.com or ecowise.com). For more information, log on to www.greenerpenny.com.

To see if there's such a facility in your area, go to **www.findacomposter.com or bpiworld.org.**

Thus far, San Francisco is the only city that picks up compostable plastics curbside, although other cities are considering it. Check with your municipal solid waste department. To find them, see the city government pages in your phone book or search by state at www.epa.gov/reg3wcmd/solidwastecontacts.htm. (See www.earth911.com.)

BEST PLASTICS FOR PICNICS AND PACKING LUNCHES

No worries about landfills when you pack reusable, BPA-free tableware and lidded food containers made from 100 percent recycled #5 plastic. Buy Recycline brand in apple green, red, or blue (www.preserveproducts.com).

Laptop Lunches sells colorful non-PVC, non-PC "bento" boxes—lidded plastic trays containing four removable boxes that keep your courses separate. Plus stainless fork and spoon, and vacuum jar to keep foods hot or cold (www.laptoplunches.com).

Life Without Plastic offers a more traditional wood bento box, as well as sandwich-size, stainless steel food boxes (www.lifewithoutplastic.com).

Lunch On the Go makes nifty #5 plastic bento boxes, sold at www.greenfeet.com, where you can also find soy-wax paper sandwich bags.

Reusable Bags also sells a variety of safe plastic and lightweight stainless bento boxes (www.reusablebags.com).

For more information, see the "GreenerPenny's Better Bottles Shopping List" in chapter 1.

Food Storage and Cookware

BISPHENOL A IN CANNED FOODS

If you regularly eat canned food, or have an infant who drinks formula, here's something you should know: almost all can linings contain BPA, and it's been shown to migrate into the food at normal shelf temperatures.

The good news: Only about 11 percent of canned products ever have levels approximating the exposure that have harmed animals in lab tests. And, really, not to worry, because there are some very easy ways you can reduce your exposure, as follows.

Avoiding Canned BPA

The following actions will help you avoid exposing yourself or your family to harmful levels of BPA:

- Eat more fresh and frozen foods and less food from cans.

- Choose preserved foods, such as spaghetti sauce, in non-leaching glass jars or in BPA-free "aseptic" packaging (aluminum- and polyethylene-lined cartons) rather than cans. Because BPA leaches most readily into fatty and acidic foods, it's a good idea to buy foods such as tomato paste and soups in cartons like Tetra Pak's Tetra Brik, which is made with wood pulp that's certified sustainable by the ubergreen Forest Stewardship Council (FSC). See www.tetrapak.com.

- Instead of buying canned baby formula, buy it in plastic bottles, which leach less BPA, according to the Environmental Working Group. Or buy powdered formula—BPA hasn't been found to leach into dry food from cans—and add water as directed.

- If you need to buy canned beans or vegetables, consider products from Eden Organics, which uses BPA-free cans (except for its tomato products).

> See
> **www.edenorganics.com.**

- No need to toss the canned foods already in your pantry! But do eat 'em up sooner rather than later, since the longer they sit around, the more BPA may infiltrate the contents. By the same reasoning, when buying canned foods, choose those with the most distant expiration date, because they'll be newest, and least exposed to BPA.

- Keep canned foods away from heat, which encourages leaching. For instance, don't store them in a cupboard next to the stove or a radiator.

- Canned sodas and juices have shown much lower BPA levels than foods, but again, you can easily reduce exposure by buying drinks in glass or non-leaching PET (#1) or HDPE (#2) plastic bottles.

> For more information, see the Environmental Working Group's excellent BPA summary and timeline: **www.ewg.org/reports/bpatimeline**.

NONSTICK COOKWARE?

By now, most people have heard some unsavory rumors about "Teflon" chemicals used in some nonstick coatings for pots and pans—and in pizza boxes, microwave popcorn bags, and rain and stain treatments such as Scotchgard. At least one of these rumors is true: When overheated (above 500°F) these nonstick coatings can release hazardous fumes. These fumes have killed pet birds. They can also cause flulike symptoms in people.

How to know if something is heated over 500°F: Although it's hard to measure, a good rule of thumb is not to leave a pot on the largest burner over the highest flame, which would cause the food to burn or boil over, anyway.

Food Storage and Cookware

The culprits are a family of chemicals known as perfluorochemicals. Perfluorooctanoic acid (PFOA) is used in the manufacture of the nonstick chemical polytetrafluoroethylene (PTFE), used in Teflon, Silverstone, and similar nonstick coatings. PFOA has been linked to certain cancers, and it can interfere with normal fetal development.

PFOA manufacturer DuPont and other companies that use the chemical have voluntarily agreed to phase it out entirely by 2015. But PFOA and other perfluorochemicals continue to collect in the environment, including in our drinking water and our bodies. In addition, some of the new perfluorochemicals with which they may be replaced have shown some troubling traits, such as being toxic to aquatic animals.

So, what to do about nonstick pans?

Relax. Odds are a Teflon skillet isn't going to cause you any harm. Tests show that there's very little release of perfluorochemicals from consumer products, including cookware—if it's used as intended, and the coating is not damaged. But there are two reasons for phasing out your Teflon pan if it gets scorched or scratched, and choosing a safer material for its replacement.

First, the Teflon chemicals are getting into our bodies somehow, so it's better for the planet and our health if perfluorochemicals get phased out as quickly as possible. One way to do this is to cut consumer demand by simply not buying the stuff.

Second, cooking is full of accidental overheatings, to put it mildly, so it makes sense to use durable cookware that won't put pets or people—or that bird outside the window—at risk of inhaling toxic fumes.

This said, am I recommending you toss your Teflon? Not if it's in good working order. Just follow these tips for using it more safely.

Teflon Safe Use Tips

Use nonstick cooking surfaces gently, stirring and turning foods with non-scratching wood, silicone, or, yes, Teflon utensils.

GreenerPenny's Tips

RECOMMENDED POTS AND PANS

Ready for a new pot or pan? The following types of cookware will not release toxic fumes:

CRATE & BARREL'S MARIO BATALI ENAMEL:(www.crateandbarrel.com).

CUISINART GREEN GOURMET: The company gives assurances that their Thermolon nonstick coating is free of PFOA and PTFE. A pleasure to cook with, the skillet retains heat well and makes for perfectly fried and flipped eggs and omelettes (www.amazon.com).

GREENPAN: The company president vouches that his nonstick coating doesn't use PFOA or PTFE. A nice lightweight pan (www.target.com).

LE CREUSET ENAMEL COOKWARE: The black satin surface in their skillets, which looks like cast iron, is actually silky black nonstick enamel. Great stuff! (www.lecreuset.com).

LODGE CAST IRON COOKWARE: These cast-iron classics now come pre-seasoned, and are virtually nonstick—and indestructible (www.lodgemfg.com).

For more information, log on to www.greenerpenny.com.

II. A *Green* and Healthy Home

Homeowners can save with federal tax credits and, in some states, utility rebates for energy-saving home improvements.

ONE GREEN THING

Wash most of your laundry in cold water.

Why? Cold water uses about 90 percent less energy than hot, according to the U.S. Department of Energy. If every household in the United States washed four out of five loads in cold water instead of hot, we'd prevent almost 50 million tons of carbon emissions a year—which would have the same effect as taking 10 million cars off the road.

ANOTHER GREEN THING

Hang it all! As much as possible, dry your laundry on a rack or line instead of by machine.

Why? While the dryer is not the most power-draining appliance—that distinction belongs to the refrigerator, which is constantly running—it is the most energy-intensive when turned on. Every time you hang-dry a load of laundry instead, you save 4.4 pounds of carbon emissions. Ninety percent of U.S. households have dryers, each of which does an average four hundred loads a year. If every U.S. household let just one load of laundry air-

> Plus, when you hang-dry your laundry, you're burning calories, bending and stretching, breathing fresh air. If you do this every day, who needs yoga class?

dry, it would save 250,000 tons of CO$_2$—providing the same effect as taking 50,000 cars off the road.

GreenerPenny's *Tips*

TOP PRODUCTS FOR HANGING LAUNDRY

Drying racks made of New England white pine and birch, from second-growth forests and rescued mill scraps (www.abundantearth.com)

Clothesline kits using Vermont cedar poles (www.smartdrying.com)

Certified organic hemp clothesline ropes (up to 108 feet long, with varying thickness) (www.rawganique.com)

Clothespins made from recycled plastic, packaged in a hemp bag ($14 at www.projectlaundrylist.org)

For more information, log on to www.greenerpenny.com.

Appliances

most-asked question

No. You can save significant energy, carbon, and money without buying a new machine by making the choices in the "Choose It/Lose It" table below.

> Use your washer's fastest spin speed; the more water removed, the less drying time (and energy) will be needed. (Note: Front-loading washers have the fastest spinning capacity.) Use auto dry cycles instead of timed drying.

WASHER/ DRYER TIPS

choose it	lose it
Wash most loads in cold water.	Wash most loads in hot water.
Wash very soiled loads in warm water, reserving hot water for killing dust mites in bedding every two weeks. Switching your temperature setting from hot to warm reduces energy use by 50 percent.	
Always rinse in cold water.	Rinse in warm or hot water.
Wash and dry only full-capacity loads. (This reduces the total number of loads.)	Run washer or dryer with small loads.
Hang at least one load a week to dry.	Routinely dry by machine.

Do One Green Thing

84

better for your health

Electricity generation is the highest greenhouse-gas-emitting sector in the United States, at 34 percent. Buildings, including our homes, consume up to 76 percent of total U.S. electricity, and emit 43 percent of GHG. By using less energy at home, we reduce emissions of CO_2, the principal greenhouse gas, which is released from power plants that burn fossil fuels to supply us with electricity. Dialing back global warming is a win-win proposition for human health.

In 2009, for the first time, the Environmental Protection Agency classified greenhouse gases as air pollution, stating that they pose hazards to human health in particular, because hotter weather produces more smog, a cause of asthma attacks and lung cancer. Power plants also emit tiny particulates, or soot, and toxic chemicals known as polycyclic aromatic hydrocarbons (PAHs), which have been connected to impaired development in newborns. Finally, power plants also emit the toxic mercury that gets into our fish!

For more studies on how global warming threatens human health, see the Harvard Center for Health and the Global Environment **(www.chge.med.harvard.edu).**

better for the planet

Your household has an energy carbon footprint, which is the amount of greenhouse gas (GHG) released by the burning of fossil fuels in power plants to fill your energy needs. Typical U.S. households are responsible for 16,200 pounds of GHG from electricity use, and 11,000 if they use natural gas, says the EPA. According to McKinsey & Co., a global economic research institute, Americans' greatest potential for reducing greenhouse gas emissions is by conserving energy in the residential sector. It's so easy they call it the "low-hanging fruit."

So pluck the fruit! Every little step we make to reduce our carbon footprint—such as washing in cold water, running fewer loads in the dryer, turning off lights when they're not in use, and replacing incandescent lightbulbs with efficient ones—collectively adds up to curbing climate change.

better for the budget

The average U.S. household spends about $2,000 a year on electricity and heating fuel. You'll save up to $20 a year by washing in cold or warm instead of hot water. If you hang-dry just *half* of your annual laundry load—say, in the warm half of the year—you can reduce GHG emissions by an average of 723 pounds and save about $50 a year.

Electricity generation is the highest greenhouse-gas-emitting sector in the United States.

If I can only afford one new laundry machine, should it be a washer or dryer?

A washer, for which green standards exist. You can buy an energy- and water-efficient washing machine that qualifies for the EPA's blue Energy Star label. There is no green label for dryers, because they're all basically energy hogs.

When you're ready to replace an old top-loading machine, consider an Energy Star front-loading model, which can use as little as a third as much energy.

LAUNDRY APPLIANCE SHOPPING TIPS

Washing Machines

As a general rule, front-loading washers are generally more energy- and water-efficient than top loaders, but you can find top savers in each category.

Look for a model that bears both an Energy Star label and a Water Efficient Factor of less than 9.5 (which means it uses 35 to 50 percent less water than an average washer). An Energy Star–approved model has to be at least 50 percent more energy efficient than standard models, and can save you more than $145 a year compared with a ten-year-old machine. See www.energystar.gov.

Keep shopping! Energy Star is just the baseline, and there are many washing machines that reach well beyond the EPA standard to provide much bigger savings.

Check the websites of the Consortium for Energy Efficiency **(www.ceel.org)** *and* Consumer Reports **(www.consumerreports.org),** *which regularly list the tip-top among the latest electricity- and water-saving appliance crop.*

Clothes Dryers

Consider choosing a gas model, which produces only about 40 percent of the carbon emissions caused by an electric dryer, according to *Consumer Reports*.

Choose a dryer with a moisture sensor, which shuts the machine off when the clothes are dry. It costs about $50 more, but it will reduce emissions by 10 percent and repay you in lower energy bills and less shrinkage and damage to clothes, according to the American Council for an Energy Efficient Economy (www.aceee.org).

SAVE BIG WITH ENERGY STAR APPLIANCES AND ELECTRONICS

In 2007 alone, by purchasing Energy Star products and otherwise using energy efficiently, Americans saved more than $16 billion on their utility bills while reducing greenhouse gas emissions equal to those from 27 million vehicles.

Homeowners can save with federal tax credits and, in some states, utility rebates for energy-saving home improvements such as using weather stripping, installing solar power systems, and buying some Energy Star appliances, including refrigerators, washing machines, water heaters, and air conditioners.

See
www.energy.gov/taxbreaks.htm
to find out if your state gives rebates for energy efficiency;
also, search the database at
www.dsireusa.org.

CALCULATE YOUR CARBON FOOTPRINT

Several online calculators are available to help you determine your annual production of CO_2, or carbon "footprint." They take into account specific lifestyle choices that either add CO_2 to the atmosphere or reduce it.

To calculate your household's emissions, go to www.epa.gov/climatechange /emissions/ind_calculator. To add up your overall transportation and household emissions, go to www.carbonfund.org. Also, see the calculator at the website of Al Gore's *An Inconvenient Truth*, www.climatecrisis.net/takeaction/carboncalculator/.

To get more carbon footprint reduction tips, a great place to start is Union of Concerned Scientists **(www.ucsusa.org/globalwarming).**

If every U.S. home replaced one
standard incandescent bulb with a
CFL, we'd collectively conserve enough
energy to light 3 million
homes for a year.

Lighting

7

ONE GREEN THING

**Switch to a green lightbulb.
(Yes, you've heard this before,
but there's a good reason.)**

*Why? Lighting really is the quickest, easiest
way to make a huge energy-saving difference.
Replace just one incandescent bulb with an
Energy Star-approved, efficient compact
fluorescent light (CFL) bulb. Already been*

there, done that? Replace an incandescent with one of the new, even longer-lasting, light-emitting diodes (LEDs), the next green thing in lightbulbs.

Lighting accounts for 20 percent of our energy use, according to the EPA. If every U.S. home replaced one standard incandescent bulb with a CFL, the savings would be equivalent to keeping the greenhouse gas emissions of 800,000 cars out of our atmosphere. We'd collectively conserve enough energy to light 3 million homes for a year, and save about $600 million.

> **In two to three months (or after eight hundred light hours), around the time a regular bulb burns out, your CFL will still be shining strong—illuminating ten times longer than an incandescent. An LED will shine twenty-five times longer than a regular bulb!**

A CFL illuminates ten times longer than an incandescent bulb.

Don't CFLs cast an ugly, greenish fluorescent light that's unflattering and hard on the eyes?

These days, if you pick the right CFL for the task or atmosphere you seek, whether it's reading, cooking, dining, or grooming, you won't notice any difference from an energy-draining incandescent bulb. How to choose the right CFL? Energy Star CFLs nowadays must have a color rating index (CRI) of at least 80, approaching daylight's full spectrum of 100. And the EPA is now more closely vetting manufacturers who boast these ratings.

You can choose a CFL in a clear bluish white color that's comparable to daylight, or a soft yellow/red, resembling the light of an incandescent. LEDs, which aren't fluorescents at all, can now be found in bulbs that shine as bright and warm as incandescents.

GREEN LIGHTING

choose it

Energy Star–approved* CFL light-bulbs and fixtures

Energy Star–approved* LED lamps and fixtures

*Look for the blue label with the star.

lose it

Incandescent lightbulb

better for your health

CFLs and LEDs are cool. While incandescents waste up to 95 percent of their energy as heat, which in turn warms the air around them, heat represents only 30 percent of a CFL's output, and LEDs, the coolest of all, remain at room temperature while illuminated. These energy-efficient bulbs are less likely to burn you if touched or brushed against, and your home will stay more comfortable, with less air-conditioning needed in the summer.

better for the planet

And how! CFLs are 75 percent more efficient and last ten times longer than incandescents (about nine years, if illuminated three hours a day). LEDs, light-emitting diodes, now made in standard lightbulb form, are three times more efficient than CFLs, and they last up to ten times longer than CFLs, and one hundred times longer than regular bulbs. LEDs are mercury-free.

better for the budget

While CFLs cost more initially, each one saves you between $30 and $47 in energy costs and an average 700 pounds of CO_2 over their long life-spans, compared with incandescent bulbs. And CFLs keep coming down in price. A decade ago they averaged $11 per bulb. Now they can be widely bought for $3 to $6 each, or for as low as $6.99 for a four-pack. "A typical household can retrofit incandescent bulbs with CFL fixtures and get payback in less than a year," McKinsey and Co. reports.

Right now, LED bulbs are a lot more expensive, starting at about $30 each (gulp!), but that bulb will save you $200 over its average twenty-five years. They're also rapidly going down in price. And a table or floor lamp that's designed for, and comes with, an LED bulb can be priced competitively with new conventional models.

another question

To find out where to take your used CFLs, go to www.earth911.com.

I've heard that CFLs contain mercury and have to be recycled in a special way. Won't this cause me a lot of time and trouble?

It's true that CFLs include a tiny amount of mercury, which can be released when the lightbulbs are broken, but since new industry regulations went into effect in 2007, the amount of mercury in CFLs has shrunken to an average four milligrams, compared with the five hundred milligrams found in old thermometers. Unlike those thermometers, if a CFL is broken, only 14 percent of the mercury it contains is released. The rest sticks to the inside of the bulb.

It is also true that CFLs are not currently included in curbside recycling. But they shouldn't inconvenience you any more than would taking recyclable bottles back to stores. Several retailers of CFLs, including all IKEA and Home Depot stores, and many hardware and lighting chains, accept used CFLs for safe recycling. Or you can drop them off at your municipal household hazardous waste facility.

Bottom line? Compared with fish, the amount of mercury in CFLs is insignificant; not to mention, we don't eat lightbulbs! Plus, CFLs help keep mercury out of fish. That said, there's still a lot of wiggle room for more mercury reduction in CFLs, and some CFLs manufacturers are voluntarily using only one milligram of this toxic heavy metal, well below the EPA's ceiling of five milligrams per CFL bulb.

Lighting

If you want to maximize your CFL's or LED's glow, you can choose a fixture that's specifically made for it—but you don't have to buy an Energy Star–qualified fixture. You can insert a CFL into almost any standard lamp base or fixture. Just choose the equivalent incandescent wattage as noted on the CFL package. The exception: CFLs should not be completely enclosed; they need to "breathe" or they'll go on the blink.

Having tested quite a few CFL and LED bulbs, I have concluded that what you see and like is largely a matter of personal taste, so try a variety of different bulbs from the lists here. Your preference will also depend on what you want to illuminate: desk top, kitchen counter, bathroom mirror, your bed for reading. The quality of CFLs is generally so high that the specialists I queried, designer David Bergman of Cyberg Designs, and Eric Paige, lighting engineer at the University of California, Davis, declined to specify a preference for any particular bulb.

Energy Star–qualified CFL fixtures include table lamps, sconces, ceiling lamps, and track lighting. For LEDs, qualified fixtures include under-the-shelf fixtures, cabinet and closet lighting, and outdoor fixtures. Energy Star is a bit behind the times with regard to the new crop of table, desk, and floor lamps designed specifically for LEDs, which haven't been rated yet.

CHOOSING A CFL

First, make sure it's an Energy Star CFL. It's required to have brighter, warmer light, and will reach full brightness more quickly, too, within three minutes of being switched on.

Look on the packaging or on the bulb itself for its correlated color temperature,

CFLs*

Earthmate

MaxLite

Feit Ecobulb

Philips with Alto

Litetronics

Sylvania

FOR LIGHT QUALITY

Task or day lighting: BlueMax, MaxLite

Soft white: n:vision (four bulbs for $10 at Home Depot)

Desk/reading light: Philips with Alto

Warm ambient or overhead lighting: GE Soft White or Lights of America Mini Twister

For a full list of CFLs and fixtures (search by zip code), see www.energy star.gov. For some lovely CFL fixtures, see David Bergman's lamps at www.cyberg.com. For more information see Environmental Defense's Lightbulb Selector at www.edf.org.

CFLs are also available in dimmer bulbs, including by MaxLite.

*Lowest-mercury brands listed in order from lowest to highest levels, but all have less than 2.7 milligrams. Source of mercury level information: EWG's lightbulb shopping guide, at www.ewg.org/greenlightbulbs. For more information, log on to www.greenerpenny.com.

FOR "COLOR"

or CCT, measured in kelvins (K). The majority of "soft" or "warm white" CFLs are 2700–3000 K, which is comparable to the light of an incandescent. If you want a bright, blue "daylight" look, choose kelvins of 3500–6500 or higher, the EPA advises.

LIGHT-EMITTING DIODES (LEDs)

The field is still narrow, although LEDs will ultimately win the day as the greenest home lighting option. For more information, see "Better for Your Health" and "Better for the Planet" about lightbulbs on pages 94.

WHAT TO DO IF A CFL BREAKS

Don't panic! Air out the room, leaving it for about ten minutes, until mercury vapor condenses into little drops. Wearing gloves and covering your nose and mouth, pick up the broken glass and put it in a lidded jar. Wipe up the mercury drops thoroughly with a damp rag and sticky tape. Wrap up the rags and jar, seal all in a plastic bag, and take it to the nearest hazardous waste site (see www.epa.gov/epa waste/hazard or www.earth911.com). Continue ventilating the room.

For more detailed instructions, see www.ewg.org.

Safe CFL handling tip: Never screw in a lightbulb by holding the glass, which could break; always hold the bulb by its base.

QUICK HOME ENERGY SAVINGS CHECKLIST

Heating and Cooling

Heating (31 percent) and cooling (12 percent) are the biggest energy drain in the home. Reduce that drain by taking the following steps:

- Monitor the thermostat. In winter, try to keep temperatures to at least 68°F by day and 60°F overnight. With electric heat, you'll save 236 pounds of carbon for every degree you go beneath 70. With gas heat, you'll save 320 pounds. In summer, set the air-conditioner at no lower than 78°F. Every degree you go above 72 reduces GHG by 121 pounds.

- When you buy an air-conditioner, make sure it's Energy Star (www.energy star.gov).

- Treat your windows to some energy-saving dressing. Inexpensive blinds, shades, or curtains reduce cooling bills in summer and heating bills in winter. See the U.S. Department of Energy's tips on shades at www1.eere.energy.gov/consumer/tips/windows. Save even more money in the long run with insulated window shades or Low-e (low-emissivity) glass coatings, simple films that you can apply to panes yourself. See www.snaptint.com. If you're building new, or ready to replace windows, choose Energy Star Low-e, double-glazed models. See www.energystar.gov and www.buildinggreen.com.

The Refrigerator

Appliances use 17 percent of the average home's energy. The refrigerator alone uses 8 percent! You can reduce GHG by up to 700 pounds a year with the following easy refrigerator maintenance:

- Keep the refrigerator thermostat at 36–38°F and the freezer at 3°F.

- Don't let clutter accumulate on top of your fridge, which makes it work harder and burn more electricity. For the same reason, clean the refrigerator coils at least once a year. (Remember to *unplug the fridge first,* so you don't shock yourself!) You can use a handheld vacuum or a regular vacuum with a hose and crevice attachment to vacuum the thick, caked-on dust from the coils. But to really dislodge the dust, use a refrigerator coil brush, available at home supply stores.

- Keep the fridge away from heat sources, such as the stove.

- Keep the freezer full, and be sure to cool hot foods a bit before refrigerating them.

- Is your fridge leaking cold air? Close a dollar bill in the door—if it stays put, your seal is energy tight and your food is safe. If it slides down, it's time to replace the gasket. (Quite a production, I'm afraid, but there are helpful tips on how to do this at www.ehow.com/how_8259_replace-gasket-refrigerator.html.)

- Time for a new fridge? The first requirement is that it be Energy Star–approved, which means it must use about 15 percent less energy than conventional new fridges, and 40 percent less than pre-2001 models. Energy Star can reduce carbon emissions by more than 500 pounds and save you up to $70 a year. See www.energystar.gov/. But don't stop there! Look for fridges that use 20 to 30 percent less energy than those with comparable specs (size, freezer position, etc.). The Energy Guide label on appliances rates a model's efficiency. Check the yearly kilowatt hours; the lower that number, the higher your savings.

Which is the most energy efficient, a fridge with its freezer on the top, bottom, or side?

Top freezers use the least energy on average, according to the EPA, followed by bottom-mounted ones. Side-by-side configurations use the most. See www.greenerchoices.org.

The Stove and Oven

There are no Energy Star–approved stoves, for the same reason as there are none for dryers—they're hot! But there are real energy-saving differences among types. The most efficient stove: one with an electric-induction cooktop, which can save up to 40 percent of the energy used by standard stoves. The second most efficient: gas stoves, especially ones with electric ignitions rather than pilot lights.

The most efficient oven option? The microwave, by far. Next most efficient is the convection oven, which saves 20 percent compared with the energy used by a conventional oven.

ENERGY-SAVING COOKING TIPS

Reduce cooking time with heavy-bottomed, high-conductivity cookware that heats quickly and holds heat: copper-bottom stainless pans and enameled cast-iron.

Use lids to keep heat from escaping. Also, don't preheat the oven for more than five minutes.

The Dishwasher

If you're looking for a new dishwasher (a good idea if your present machine is more than 10 years old), first make sure it's Energy Star. For models, see www.energy

star.gov. Next, read the yellow Energy Guide label looking for an Energy Factor of at least 0.65, which is about 40 percent better than the federal standard, according to ACEEE. Finally, check the water efficiency, which can vary up to 50 percent between Energy Star models alone! Ask the salesperson, or look for water usage info on the manufacturer's pamphlet. Most newer models use about 7–10 gallons per load, but some water-efficient machines consume as little as 4.5 gallons per load. All told, an Energy Star dishwasher can save you $25 a year.

Maximize your dishwasher's efficiency with these usage tips:

- Scrape food off dishes rather than prerinsing, and save up to 20 gallons per load.
- Run full loads.
- Keep dishwasher on air-dry rather than heat-dry cycle

What saves more energy and water, machine- or hand-washing dishes?

Using the dishwasher. On average, a modern machine uses only half the electricity and a mere one-sixth of the water that hand-washing does, according to a thorough, seven-country study of dishwashing habits by the University of Bonn, Germany. Some new dishwashers can save 4,300 gallons a year over hand-washing. But if you don't have a dishwasher (I must confess that my husband and I have *never* owned one), you can still save energy and water with these simple tips:

- Apply the full-load rule to hand-washing: Scrape dishes clean, and let them soak in a sink or dishpan.

- Scrub dishes, drinkware, and cutlery, stack them to one side, then rinse them in a clean dishpan, giving them a final quick pass under the aerated tap (rinse cutlery by the handful, not one by one).

- Buy a low-flow faucet aerator for your sink. Standard faucets release 2.2 gallons per minute (gpm). An aerator can go as low as 0.5 gpm; available at most hardware stores or www.greenfeet.com.

Electronics and Gadgets

Plug everything you can—computer, printer, television, VCR, music player, cell phone charger—into power strips and switch them off when you go out or go to sleep. Whether off or on, electronics products continue draining power from the socket.

How much can they drain? A lot. Over its lifetime, 70 percent of a TV's energy is consumed while it's turned off. Here's what you can lose every day: 672 KwH through the TV, and 336 KwH through your VCR.

COMPUTERS

Set your computer to go into sleep mode when you take a break for fifteen minutes or more. This will reduce its power use from 60 watts (flat-monitor desktop) or 30 watts (laptop) to about 5 watts. When you take long breaks, be sure to turn your computer off, which saves still more energy.

another question

What's greener, a laptop or a desktop?

A laptop, because it's smaller, and hence uses fewer materials and natural resources, and it's more energy efficient. On average, a laptop uses only 15 to 25 watts versus the 150 watts consumed by a desktop and monitor.

CHECKLIST FOR A NEW COMPUTER

When it's time to purchase a new computer, make sure:

- It's energy efficient/ Energy Star–compliant;

- It has a high (silver or gold) ranking from the Electronic Product Environmental Assessment Tool (EPEAT);

- Its manufacture minimized the use of hazardous chemicals, toxic heavy metals, and PVC plastic; and

- Its manufacturer has a responsible take-back/recycling program and is involved in reducing greenhouse gas emissions.

> If all computers sold in the United States met the U.S. EPA's Energy Star standards, we'd save about $2 billion in electricity each year, and reduce the same amount of greenhouse gas emissions as taking 2 million cars off the road.

GREENER COMPUTERS
AND CELL PHONES

When you're in the market for a computer, a game console, or a cell phone, check out Greenpeace's Guide to Greener Electronics (www.greenpeace.org/international/campaigns/toxics/electronics/how-the-companies-line-up), which is thoughtfully updated four times a year. This top watchdog organization rates every computer maker based on its use of toxic materials, the energy its products consume, the greenhouse gases and e-waste it releases in manufacturing, its products' energy efficiency, and its recycling and take-back programs.

Hazardous components in computers and other electronics include: arsenic, lead, mercury, toxic flame retardants, and PVC plastic, which releases toxic phthalates (see pages 81 and 126).

Brominated flame retardants (BFRs) include polybrominated diphenyl ethers (PBDEs), which have been implicated in reproductive and neurological problems in animal tests, and are found in high levels in the breast milk of American women. The Environmental Working Group has a list of PDBE-free computers with links to manufacturers' websites, at www.ewg.org/pbdefree.

That said, some popular computer brands, although they scored low in Greenpeace's rankings, are still pretty green—which shows how much progress is being made in this sector.

Hazardous components in computers lead, mercury, toxic flame retardants.

ENERGY-SAVING HIGH-TECH GADGETS

- A push-button gadget that plugs into your PC can save you $50 a year by putting your computer to sleep whenever you wander away or catnap (www.eco-button/usa.com).

- A solar charger (it can be plugged into an electrical wall outlet, too, if needed) by Solio can charge your cell phone, MP3 player, PDA, camera, GPS, game player (www.amazon.com).

- Smart power strips sense whether your computer or TV is actively running or on standby, and if it's the latter, they turn themselves off. Check 'em out at www.smarthomeusa.com and www.byebyestandby.com.

- Measure the wattage drain of your electronics and appliances and get motivated to dial it back with the Kill-a-Watt (www.thinkgeek.com/gadgets).

- Get a read-out on your whole home energy use and costs with the Power Monitor (www.blackanddecker.com).

and other electronics include: arsenic, and PVC plastic.

Conserving water helps all of

us to build a reservoir of clean

water for our future.

Saving Water

8

ONE GREEN THING

Take a shorter shower.

Why? Seventy-five percent of residential water consumption takes place in the bathroom, and the shower is the third greatest water hog in a home (after the toilet and clothes washing machine). Plus, while you can wash clothes in cold water, showers are generally taken hot, and thus consume energy for heating the water.

Which uses more water, taking a shower or a bath?

A bath, actually. An average shower lasts eight minutes and runs through 17.2 gallons of water, according to the Alliance for Water Efficiency. The average bath, on the other hand, consumes 20–45 gallons of water, depending on whether you fill the tub halfway or to the brim (or keeping adding a little more hot water as you soak, which I'm guilty of). But, overall, the shower's a bigger hog, because it's used more frequently.

SAVING WATER

choose it

Take a shower instead of a bath.

Keep showers to five minutes or less. The energy expended for a daily five-minute shower is responsible for emitting 855 pounds of CO_2 a year—513 pounds less than an eight-minute shower.

Use a low-flow showerhead that runs through less than 2 gallons per minute (gpm).

Turn off the water when you soap yourself and shampoo; turn it back on to rinse.

Turn down your hot water heater thermostat to 120°F.

lose it

Don't make tub baths a regular thing (but do enjoy the occasional indulgence).

Don't take an eight-minute shower. An eight-minute daily shower is responsible for emitting 1,368 pounds of CO_2 a year.

Don't use a showerhead with a 2.5–5 gallons-per-minute flow. Although new U.S.-made showerheads cannot release more than 2.5 gpm, older models are made to release more.

Don't keep your water heater at 130–140°F, the energy-wasting national average.

better for your health

The UN predicts that two thirds of us, worldwide, will face water scarcity by 2025. Although most of the 1.1 billion people (16 percent of the world's population) who currently lack clean drinking water live in the poorest nations, Americans are not invulnerable. Water shortages are expected in thirty-six of the states by 2013. Conserving water helps all of us to build a reservoir—sort of like a bank—of clean water for our future. In the United States, the water we shower and flush the toilet with is the same water we drink. Once that clean water goes down the drain, it's waste water.

We also shouldn't overlook the personal health benefits: The American Academy of Dermatology advises keeping showers short, because long, hot showers are a common cause of dry, itchy skin. And washing your hair too frequently dries it out.

Turning down your water heater thermostat to 120°F will also prevent scalding.

better for the planet

Showers in the United States send 1.2 trillion gallons of water down the drain every year. Simply shortening yours, you'll save water, a dwindling resource. Global warming will lead to more water shortages, according to the International Panel on Climate Change. Pollution also reduces the amount of clean water we can use at any given time. While the world's supply of clean water is finite, our population, agriculture, and industry continue to grow and consume unsustainable amounts. The more water we conserve, the more clean water will be available for all of us, including aquatic ecosystems, which contain some of the most sensitive life on the planet.

You'll also reduce your household's contribution to global warming. Turn your water heater thermostat down from the standard 130°F to 120°F, and reduce carbon emissions by an average 733 pounds a year, says Consumers Union. On average, heating water for each shower minute means that 204 pounds of carbon were emitted by fossil fuels burned in the power plant that supplied your electricity. If your conventional hot water heater uses natural gas, which emits less carbon than coal or petroleum, each shower minute is the equivalent of about 93 pounds of CO_2 emissions. A tankless natural gas water heater would give additional savings, but best of all would be a zero-emissions solar water heater. With our national commitment to renewable energy, there are lots of new, increasingly affordable possibilities for solar hot water.

For more about water heaters, see www.epa.gov/energystar.

better for the budget

 By cutting down on your hot water consumption, you can look forward to the following savings:

- If you're using a regular showerhead, every minute you shave off your shower will save you about $17 a year per person, based on current national averages for the cost of electricity per kilowatt hour. In a four-person household, that's an average savings of $68 a year per minute.

- If you take a five-minute instead of eight-minute shower, you'll save $51 per year per person, and $204 for a family of four.

- A low-flow showerhead that releases about 1.5 gpm can save you about $160 a year with electric heating and $115 with gas, according to an excellent article in the *Wall Street Journal,* "How to Go Green in Hard Times," in February 2009.

GreenerPenny's *Favorite*

WATER-SAVING SHOWER SUPPLIES

- Delta's H2O Kinetics 1.6 gpm showerhead uses about one-third less water per minute than the 2.5 gpm showerhead the federal government requires, but it's designed so that the water droplets are larger and therefore retain more heat. We use one at home, and the water pressure feels fine. See www.deltafaucet.com.

- Moen also makes low-flow showerheads, averaging 1.75 gpm. While low-flow showerheads start at about $30, and the Delta Kinetic costs $50 and change, the payback in lower energy and water bills is quick. Plus, check with your utility company, which may provide you with a rebate for a low-flow showerhead.

- For those who don't wear a waterproof watch with a second hand, little hourglass shower timers, for four- or five-minute showers, are sold for less than $5 at www.greenfeet.com. Apply to the wall with a suction cup and dial or invert to start the trickle of sand. Or go to your local hardware or household supply store and buy a windup egg timer with a bell, which can provide some fun and even excitement if you're cooking an egg at the same time (which provides incentive to get out of the shower).

For more information, log on to www.greenerpenny.com.

Water the lawn and garden in the evening or early morning to prevent evaporation.

THE WATER-SENSIBLE TOILET, AT LAST

No surprise, the toilet is the biggest water guzzler in the American home. An average 30 percent of the water we draw indoors goes down the toilet. The average American flushes 140,000 times in a lifetime. And we fill our toilet tanks with the same drinking water that comes out of our taps.

Now high-efficiency Water Sense toilets are available. They use 20 percent less water than the federal standard. For models, see www.epa.gov/watersense.

If you're not ready to replace your toilet with a low-flush model, you can take the following simple steps.

Top off your tank with a sink. The SinkPositive diverts tap water to its faucet after you flush, and lets you wash your hands with fresh water *before* it fills the toilet bowl. The result: The bowl fills with "grey," or used, water instead of clean drinking water, so the same water gets used twice. See www.sinkpositive.com.

The simplest solution remains placing a filled one-liter water bottle in the tank. It will displace the same amount, saving one liter of water per flush, or about one-tenth of the average 10 liters voided by an older toilet. Or buy a "toilet tank bank" for about $2 at www.greenfeet.com.

And add to your savings by flushing less often!

> Make sure your toilet doesn't leak! You can get a free sample of a "leak detective" tracing dyes kit from **www.BrightDyes.com**.

SAVING WATER IN THE GARDEN

Half a typical U.S. household's water is used out of doors, consuming an estimated 30 billion liters of water a day. That's enough to fill 14 billion six-packs of beer, according to the Worldwatch Institute. What a waste in a thirsty world!

You'll see quick savings with the following simple steps:

Water the lawn and garden in the evening or early morning to prevent evaporation.

Add drip irrigation lines, which slowly but steadily provide water close to roots, along the bases of trees and shrubs. For how-tos, see *Organic Gardening* magazine (www.organicgardening.com). Also learn about organic gardening and water saving by downloading the excellent Northeast Organic Farming Association gardening manual at www.nofa.org.

Consider watering plants and washing cars and outdoor surfaces with rainwater collected in a barrel. If you would like to reuse "greywater" collected from sinks and showers, do it carefully with an eye to sanitation; read up on it at www.greywaterguerrillas.com/greywater.html.

Find rain barrels and drip irrigation lines at www.gardeners.com.

To protect your outdoor ecosystem, make sure you use the least-toxic personal care and cleaning products recommended in chapters 9 and 11 of this book.

Cultivate native grasses and other plants, which are best suited to your region's natural rainfall levels and soil composition. Contact your local university agricultural extension or botanical garden for help.

If every U.S. household replaced one

bottle of petroleum-based detergent

with a plant-based one, 149,000

barrels of oil could be saved.

Simple Green Housekeeping

9

ONE GREEN THING

As you use them up, replace conventional cleaning products with green formulas.

Why? No need for a drastic change. But as you phase out the hard stuff in favor of gentler, plant-based formulas, you'll breathe cleaner indoor air, free of fumes, and protect your family from toxic ingredients: Household cleaning products were the second most frequent reason for calls to U.S. poisoning centers in 2007.

If every U.S. household replaced one bottle of petroleum-based detergent with a plant-based one, 149,000 barrels of oil could be saved, enough to heat and cool 8,500 homes for a year, according to Seventh Generation.

CLEANING PRODUCTS AND INDOOR AIR

most-asked question

How can I know if a cleaning product is truly green?

Choose products from among GreenerPenny's recommended brands, or mix your own from the "green light" ingredients listed in the "Choose It/Lose It" table at right.

GREEN VERSUS TOXIC CLEANING

👍 choose it

The following list recommends ingredients for making your own cleaners. For specific directions on how to mix them up, see page 123.

SIMPLY GREEN

- Baking soda (sodium bicarbonate)
- Borax (sodium borate)*
- Cornstarch
- Hydrogen peroxide
- Lemon juice
- Liquid soap (see list of green brands on page 122)
- Plant essential oils ** (for fragrance and light disinfecting)
- Table salt
- Vegetable oil (wood cleaning, polish)
- Washing soda (sodium carbonate)*
- White vinegar (contains acetic acid)

👎 lose it

The following list of toxic tongue-twisters names the top ingredients to avoid, some of which are sudsing agents/surfactants (S) and solvents/degreasers (D):

- Alkylphenol ethoxylates (APEs) and Nonyphenols (NPEs) (S)
- Ammonia
- Fragrance (which may contain toxic phthalates)
- Glycol ethers, including 2-butoxyethanol and 2-(2-methoxyethoxy) ethanol (D)
- Lye (sodium hydroxide)
- Monoethanolamine (MEA)
- Phosphates
- Sodium lauryl sulfate (S)
- Terpenes (aromatic plant oils of citrus or pine)
- Triclosan/tricloban (synthetic antibacterials)
- Any product labeled "poison," "danger," "warning," "caution"[†]

*Sold in the laundry aisle.
** Sold in health food and natural body stores; certified organic at www.mountainroseherbs.com and www.nhrorganicoils.com; fairly traded at www.organicinfusions.com.
[†]Even if they don't have these warnings, keep all cleaners, even green ones, out of the reach of children.

better for your health

While we can't avoid all the pollution we encounter in our daily lives, we can easily control our exposure to unhealthy substances in cleaning products by choosing green. This is an area to make a difference in your exposure.

Non-green, conventional ingredients include volatile organic compounds (VOCs), which evaporate from products, filling your indoor air with fumes. These VOCs have been shown to cause skin, eye, nose, throat, and lung irritation; asthma attacks; headache; and dizziness; and to expose us to chemicals such as glycol ethers, which are linked to cancer and impaired fertility.

> Phthalates in synthetic fragrances are another concern. Regular home use of spray cleaners and air fresheners was associated with a 30–50 percent higher risk of asthma in a study published in 2007.

better for the planet

Using natural cleaning ingredients actually protects our drinking water as well as plants and wildlife, since conventional cleaners have ingredients that cause harm during their production, use, and disposal. For example, the production of chlorine creates dioxins, which are cancer-causing chemicals; when chlorine mixes with organic matter, such as decaying leaves, it creates toxic chemicals that can contaminate drinking water. After they're washed down the drain, APEs, especially the type known as nonyphenol (NPE), can contaminate waterways and have been found to harm fish embryos and to mess with tadpole development. One study found disinfectant and detergent components in up to 70 percent of U.S. streams.

Which cleaning products are the most toxic and best to choose in their green form?

Conventional drain, oven, and toilet bowl cleaners contain the most dangerous chemicals, according to Philip Dickey of the Washington Toxics Coalition (www.watoxics.org), so buy or make green versions of these.

Your best all-around buy, if you want a cleaner that can be a base for mixing all the rest, is liquid dish soap, the most versatile store-bought cleaning product. You can combine it with other common household ingredients (baking soda, white vinegar) to make DIY floor and window cleaners, soft scrubs, and more.

. . . we can easily control our exposure to unhealthy substances in cleaning products by choosing green.

GreenerPenny's *Favorite*
CLEANING PRODUCTS

DISH SOAP

🍃 Clorox Greenworks: This dish soap had no detectable traces of carcinogenic 1,4 dioxane in tests performed by the Organic Consumers Association in 2008, while many products billed as "natural" and "organic" were found to be contaminated, some with quite high levels.

🍃 Dr. Bronner's Castile Soap: These highly concentrated formulas come either unscented or fragranced with organic peppermint, rose, or almond.

🍃 Seventh Generation Free & Clear: This has absolutely no fragrance, and is gentle enough to use as a hand soap. One 32-ounce bottle lasts two months of intensive hand-washing of dishes—we don't have a dishwasher—and fewer suds need less water for rinsing.

TOILET BOWL CLEANER

🍃 Ecover toilet bowl cleaner: Use this for regular swishing.

🍃 Bon Ami scouring powder: Supplement your Ecover with this non-scratching cleaner.

OVEN CLEANER

🍃 Make your own: See the DIY recipes on page 123.

🍃 Bon Ami: Use this on a damp sponge.

DRAIN CLEANER

🍃 Make your own: see the DIY recipes on page 125.

🍃 Green drain openers: These are available from Naturally Yours (www.naturallyyoursclean.com) and Earth Friendly Products (www.ecos.com).

Note: For green cleaning product labels to look for, see the chart in the Laundry Detergents section. For more information, log on to www.greenerpenny.com.

DIY RECIPES FOR HOUSEHOLD CLEANING TASKS

Soft Scrub

2 cups baking soda

½ cup liquid plant-based soap (e.g., Dr. Bronner's castile)

3–4 drops vegetable oil

Mix and add water to desired consistency; store in lidded jar.

Fume-Free Oven Cleaner

2 cups baking soda

1 cup washing soda

1 teaspoon liquid plant-based soap

Water

1 tablespoon white vinegar

Do a preliminary wipe down of the oven with a scrubber, rag, and hot water to remove crust that hasn't yet stuck solid. Mix all the ingredients into a thick paste. Wearing gloves, apply thickly to oven interior. Leave on overnight. In the morning, put gloves back on and rinse and scrub with a sponge or rag.

Glass Cleaner

½ cup white vinegar

1 cup water

3–4 drops liquid plant-based soap

Mix in a spray bottle.

For more DIY ideas, see
www.womenandenvironment.org/greenclean/faqs.

Floor Cleaner (safe for wood)

1 cup white vinegar

1 gallon hot water

Mop floors. No need to rinse. For extra cleaning power, add ¼ cup liquid plant-based soap, but rinse, or slipperiness will result.

Disinfectant, Stain Remover, Mold Remover, Deodorizer

White vinegar or

Borax or

Hydrogen peroxide

Wearing gloves, apply either white vinegar, hydrogen peroxide, or a paste of borax and water to the affected area. Let sit for at least an hour, then scrub and wipe off with a brush, sponge, or rag.

Another stain removal remedy, particularly for laundry, is to presoak the item with one part lemon juice in four parts water.

Carpet/Upholstery Spot Cleaner

To absorb spills on carpets or upholstery fabric, apply corn starch to absorb, then pour on a little club soda to lift.

Toilet Bowl Cleaner

Baking soda
White vinegar
Hydrogen peroxide

Sprinkle the sides of the bowl with baking soda. Spray the vinegar until it lightly fizzes. Wait thirty minutes, then scrub. Want a stronger disinfectant on the rim, lid, and seat? Wipe with hydrogen peroxide.

Metal Polish

Use toothpaste.

Drain Cleaner

Baking soda
White vinegar
Boiling water

To keep your drain open, pour in equal parts baking soda and white vinegar, followed by the water, once a week. If the drain still clogs, use a plunger or plumber's snake to lift out whatever is stuck. Still clogged? Use an enzyme drain cleaner that eats the organic matter. Steer clear of regular drain openers based on toxic lye. Still stuck? Don't go nuts. Sometimes a pro is needed, so call a plumber to snake the drain.

Scents-ability: To any of these recipes, you can add your favorite essential oils, such as lavender, lemon, rosemary, or thyme, which can be found at your local natural food stores, or at **www.newdirectionsaromatics.com.**

HOME PRODUCTS THAT
RELEASE TOXIC VOCS

Vinyl (polyvinyl chloride, PVC)

Wherever possible, don't use vinyl shower curtains, flooring, or wall coverings, and keep PVC packaging out of your home. Studies have shown that PVC shower curtains and other home surfaces release toxic phthalates, hormone-disrupting chemicals that are easily inhaled. Phthalates have been found to provoke respiratory problems and asthma symptoms in children living in homes with vinyl surfaces.

> *Companies are responding to consumer concerns: IKEA's affordable plastic shower curtains are PVC-free. Target and Wal-Mart have both pledged to eliminate PVC from packaging used in their private brands.*

Synthetic Pesticides/Herbicides

Petroleum-derived insecticides of all kinds, whether they're organophosphates or pyrethroids, have one job to do: they attack the nervous systems of insects. Unfortunately, they do the same to humans, birds, and animals, and are especially dangerous to fetuses in utero and to infants and children, whose brains and nervous systems are rapidly developing. Organochlorine pesticides, such as the now-banned DDT, and herbicides such as atrazine, attack reproductive systems and have caused deformities in birds, fish, and amphibians. Others are linked to various cancers, or simply kill all sorts of plants and wildlife outright. Whether it's in your home or garden, you probably don't want these sorts of chemicals in the air you and your family breathe.

Alternative Pesticides

The solution? Stay calm and take preventive measures:

- Use integrated pest management (IPM), whether you're dealing with insects, fungi, or weeds. Indoors, put away food and keep kitchens clean; wipe up moisture, seal cracks and crevices, and fix leaks.

- Use the least-toxic baits, made of boric acid mixed with a little sugar and water, to kill roaches and ants. If necessary, commercial bait traps are less toxic than powders and sprays. Ants are also discouraged by peppermint castile soap.

- In the garden, use red-pepper spray or liquid soap to kill aphids, mites, and insects.

For more tips on eliminating specific pests, see the fact sheets of the Bio-Integral Resource Center (www.birc.org), the Washington Toxics Coalition (www.watoxics.org), or the Northwest Coalition for Alternatives to Pesticides (www.pesticide.org).

Outdoors, think organic lawn and garden care. See the publications of the Northeast Organic Farming Association's (NOFA) Organic Land Care (www.organiclandcare.net), the EPA's Healthy Lawn Healthy Environment booklet (www.epa.gov/pesticides/controlling/garden), and the list of practices and products provided by the National Coalition for Pesticide-Free Lawns (www.beyondpesticides.org/pesticidefreelawns).

Mattresses

Conventional mattresses, made with petroleum-based polyurethane foam, have routinely been treated with chemical fire retardants known as polybrominated diphenyl ethers, or PBDEs. Shown to cause behavioral and developmental problems in animal studies, PBDEs are pervasive in the environment, found in women's breast milk and the fat of harbor seals, and, like other VOCs, easily migrate out of products into house dust and air.

Environmental health advocates call PBDEs "the new PCBs," referring to the now-banned industrial chemicals that caused lower IQs in the children of women who ate PCB-contaminated fish. Although PVC, along with other materials containing phthalates, was effectively banned from use in mattresses for cribs and toddler beds in early 2009, it may still be present in mattresses made before that time, and new mattresses may, in addition to chemical fire retardants, be treated with water and stain repellants that can release formaldehyde, another toxic VOC.

To avoid these chemicals, you can choose a mattress made with a natural latex core padded with cotton and surrounded with wool, which is naturally water repellant and flame retardant. Look for labels that say the mattress meets the Consumer Products Safety Commission (CPSC) and State of California fire retardancy standards for mattresses. The mattress need not be made with organic cotton or wool to benefit your health; such materials are more of a benefit to the environment. Non-organic mattresses—and especially futons—are more affordable. Since crib mattresses are so much smaller, organic versions are less pricey.

If you don't want to pony up for a new green mattress, you can block a lot of VOCs—and allergenic dust mites—in your old one by encasing it in a tightly woven barrier cloth, or covering it with a wool or cotton mattress pad.

The following companies make greener mattresses and top pads without PBDEs (the $ indicates most affordable):

ACORN INNERSPRING: organic cotton and wool; from The Natural Bed Store ($)

DUXIANA: dreamy breathable latex-and-cotton top pad

EARTHSAKE: organic cotton and PureGrow wool

GREENSLEEP: organic cotton, wool, and silk

IKEA: 85 percent natural latex, cotton ($)

Also check these retailers: www.thenaturalbedroom.com, www.ecobedroom.com, and www.heartofvermont.com.

Mattress pads are not advised for cribs, which shouldn't contain any padding, but can be given extra protection with a flat wool "puddle pad," tucked *under* a fitted sheet. For extra adult luxury, choose a topper with a natural latex core.

LIFEKIND: organic cotton, natural latex

NATURAL BY COLGATE: coconut coir fiber, organic cotton, regular cotton

NATUREPEDIC: organic cotton, regular cotton, polyethylene ($)

VIVETIQUE: organic cotton and PureGrow wool

Synthetic Carpeting and Pressed Woods (Plywood, Particleboard)

What do carpets and pressed woods have in common? The formaldehyde, benzene, and other toxic VOCs used in the conventional glues that bind carpet fibers to backings and backings to floors, or that hold together thin layers of wood.

For VOC-free carpets and area rugs that are also free of formaldehyde-based moth- and stain-proofing, check out these companies:

INTERFACE CARPETS: they make carpet tiles and take them back for recycling (www.flor.com).

MOHAWK EVERSTRAND: their carpet is made from 100 percent post-consumer-recycled content, such as PET bottles (www.mohawkcarpet.com).

NATURE'S CARPET: they make untreated wool carpet with natural jute and latex backings (www.naturescarpet.com).

Formaldehyde can also make your eyes water and nose run, and cause headaches and dizziness, so it's healthiest to avoid new pressed-wood furniture, such as bookshelves, tables, and desks. Instead, look for solid woods at thrift stores and yard sales. And check out the furniture makers using both reclaimed and new wood certified according to Forest Stewardship Council (FSC) standards, in the Rainforest Alliance's guide: www.rainforest alliance.org/forestry/documents/smartguide_furniture.pdf.

Some places to start:

CRATE AND BARREL uses some FSC certified wood in its growing eco line of furniture. See www.crateandbarrel.com/eco-friendly-products.

ABC CARPET & HOME sells some furniture made of "good" wood, the store's self-developed label for products of non-endangered, well-managed forests. FSC certification is preferable, but ABC is making an honorable start. They also sell organic mattresses, Woolmark rugs made without child labor, and many other green home products. Although the stores are in New York City, you can order online from www.abchome.com.

TOP-OF-THE-LINE FURNITURE made from FSC-certified wood and untreated organic fibers can be bought or custom-made from the Q Collection, www.qcollection.com, or the new Jak Studio Collection by green interior designers Kelly LaPlante and James Saavedra. (See www.jakstudiocollection.com.)

SUSTAINABLE DESIGN and materials abound in furnishings from Design Within Reach (www.dwr.com).

FOR HOME BUILDING AND RENOVATION using pressed woods made with no-VOC glues and sustainable woods, see products certified by Scientific Certification Systems, www.scs1.com, and furniture at Green America's www.woodwise.org. Also, see the low-VOC bamboo plywood available at www.plyboo.com, and the great natural flooring materials, including linoleum, bamboo, hardwood, and cork, at Green Depot, www.greendepot.com.

Conventional Paints

This is an easy one! Most conventional paints contain VOCs such as toxic ethylene glycol. According to the EPA, paint fumes can trigger skin rashes, headaches, dizziness, nausea, fatigue, and other problems.

The answer? No- or low-VOC paints abound in as many colors and patinas, and from satin to matte, as the regular kind. Benjamin Moore's low-VOC Aura line scored third in performance among twenty-one paints, including conventional ones, in a March 2008 *Consumer Reports* test.

The following are all zero-VOC:

AFM SAFECOAT makes great paints and finishes (www.afmsafecoat.com).

ENVIROSAFE'S PAINT dries fast (www.envirosafepaint.com).

HOME DEPOT'S FRESHAIRE PAINT comes in recycled cans printed with soy-based inks (www.Homedepot.com).

MYTHIC PAINT has nice muted retro shades (www.mythicpaint.com).

YOLOCOLORHOUSE'S COLORS include a "little Yolo" line for children's rooms (www.yolocolorhouse.com).

> For more, any, and all green versions of home decorating products, visit
> **www.environmentalhomecenter.com**
> *or*
> **www.greendepot.com.**

LAUNDRY DETERGENTS

ONE GREEN THING

Choose detergent wisely! Make sure the next laundry detergent you buy is a concentrated formula.

Why? You'll save a lot of green. In the three years since Walmart began selling only concentrated laundry detergent, the company says its customers have saved more than 400 million gallons of water, 95 million pounds of plastic, 125 million pounds of cardboard, and 520,000 gallons of fuel used in transportation. That adds up to 9,700,000 pounds of CO_2 kept out of the atmosphere.

By reformulating its laundry detergents as concentrates, Procter & Gamble has cut down on the materials used in packaging by 25–40 percent. Putting less man-made material into our environment is a definite plus! And the smaller container lightens your grocery load.

How can I tell if a laundry detergent is best for the planet and gentlest to my nose and skin?

Choose plant-based, rather than petroleum-based, detergents that are free of synthetic or strong natural fragrances.

LAUNDRY DETERGENTS

👍 choose it

Choose products listing the following ingredients:

- Plant-based surfactants, or sudsing agents, made from corn, coconut oil, and grapefruit
- Specific plant essential oils for fragrance (in case of allergies, avoid strong citrus or pine oils)

👎 lose it

Avoid products with the following ingredients:

- Ethoxylated chemicals (such as sodium laureth sulfate)
- Generic claim "fragrance" (meaning synthetic)
- Phosphates
- Synthetic degreasers (glycol ethers)
- Synthetic surfactants (APEs)

theScience

better for your health

By choosing a detergent that is free of damaging ingredients, you avoid wearing the residue of strong fragrance and irritating chemicals that can be present in laundry products. Ingredients such as sodium lauryl sulfate and linear alkylate sulfonate can survive the rinse cycle and build up on clothes and bedding. Repeated contact with these irritants can provoke skin allergies and even asthma. Most of us have probably had that scratchy, itchy feeling on our skin from "freshly" washed clothes—but the last thing we need to do is use conventional fabric softeners, which contain many of the same ingredients!

> *Don't forget to look for my recommended ingredients in your fabric softeners, too (though once you switch to a detergent without irritating chemicals, you might not need fabric softener!).*

better for the planet

By purchasing laundry products that are safe for the environment, you eliminate the possible contamination of U.S. waterways. The average household does six laundry loads a week, and the wastewater goes straight down the drain. Right now, U.S. waterways are flush with detergent chemicals, the U.S. Geological Survey has found. Of special concern are nonylphenols (NPEs), which have been found to damage many kinds of ocean fish. Because detergent compounds have been found in 70 percent of North American streams, laundry soaps without NPEs are much healthier for aquatic life and, ultimately, our drinking water.

Another helpful guide to finding a laundry soap's health and environmental credentials is to look at labels (see the "Choose It/Lose It" table, at right).

Laundry detergents and cleaning products contain the same bad ingredients. For my full "Lose It" list of bad chemical ingredients to avoid, see the "Green Versus Toxic Cleaning" section on page 119.

LABELS FOR HOUSEHOLD CLEANERS

choose it

GREENERPENNY'S GOOD PENNY LABELS

Choose products with the following labels, which are verified by independent third parties. They're worth the money.

Certified Biodegradable

Cold-water, high-efficiency formula

Cradle to Cradle (C2C)

EPA Design for the Environment (dFe) Green Seal

Leaping Bunny (LB)

PCW (post-consumer-waste) recycled packaging

USDA Biopreferred

GREENISH LABELS

The following are somewhat reliable, if less rigorous, industry self-policing claims:

Biodegradable

No ammonia

No chlorine

No DEA/TEA

No sodium laureth sulfate

No synthetic detergents

Recycled packaging

lose it

BAD PENNY LABELS

Don't spend an extra cent based on the following claims of household cleaners, which are meaningless, according to the Consumers Union (www.eco-labels.org):

Cruelty-free

Eco/environmentally friendly

Eco/environmentally safe

Natural

Nontoxic

Septic tank safe

TOP LAUNDRY DETERGENT PICKS

The following laundry soaps bear good green labels and are free, at minimum, of nonylphenols and phosphates. All are two to three times concentrated.

- Biokleen Cold-Water (www.biokleen.com)
- Ecos by Earth Friendly Products Free & Clear (unscented) (www.ecos.com) ($)
- Ecover Laundry Wash, unscented (www.ecover.com) ($)
- Method Free & Clear or Fresh Air (www.methodhome.com) *
- Seventh Generation Free & Clear (unscented) (www.seventhgeneration.com) *($)
- Tide Cold Water (www.tide.com) ($)
- Vaska (www.vaskaproducts.com)

If you like a little scent, most of the products listed here also come in lightly fragranced formulas, using only plant essential oils.

*Key to label abbreviations/symbols:
dFe = EPA Design for the Environment Green Seal
$ = most affordable
* = received highest performance ratings for cold-water washing in high-energy, front-loading machines from *Consumer Reports*; but I find Seventh Generation's, for one, works just fine in a regular top-loader model.
For more information, log on to www.greenerpenny.com.

DRY CLEANING

Although 85 percent of U.S. dry cleaners still use the highly toxic solvent known as perchloroethylene, or "perc," safer, greener choices are becoming available, especially since the state of California ordered a phase out of perc to be completed by 2023.

What's wrong with perc? It's a volatile organic compound (VOC), meaning it vaporizes readily and is easily inhaled. Perc fumes are responsible for the pungent, sickly sweet smell that greets you when you enter a conventional dry cleaner's or walk past their outdoor vent. Symptoms of perc exposure can include dizziness, headache, nausea, and skin and lung irritation, according to the U.S. Environmental Protection Agency.

The International Agency for Research on Cancer (IARC) lists perc as a "probable human carcinogen."

WHAT CAN I DO TO REDUCE PERC?

Even if you never visit a dry cleaner's, you may be getting a low dose of perc, which is found in our air and drinking water nationwide. If you live or work near a dry cleaner's, and smell fumes, call your city or state department of health or environmental protection to request an inspection, or contact your state or regional Public Interest Research Group (PIRG; www.uspirg.org/about-us/the-state-pirgs).

Cleaning delicates at home

Cold-water washing by hand or on a delicate cycle will usually do the job, but there are exceptions, such as rayon. You can wash delicate wools and cashmeres by hand, or in netted bags on the cold gentle cycle.

RECOMMENDED GREEN LAUNDRY
PRODUCTS FOR DELICATE FABRICS

> *For tips on cleaning every kind of natural and synthetic material at home, see the Consumer Reports website,* **www.consumerreports.org/cro/ home-garden/news/2007/04/.**

Ecover Delicates Wash

Kookaburra wool wash

Laundress wool and cashmere shampoo

Best Alternative Commercial Dry Cleaning Methods

WET CLEANING

The EPA recommends wet cleaning, which uses water and mild detergent, as the most nontoxic and greenest cleaning choice. Search by zip code for a wet cleaner near you, or see the EPA's directory of wet cleaning businesses: www.epa.gov/dfe/ pubs/garment/gcrg/cleanguide.pdf).

> *When it comes to dry cleaning, "organic," "green," "nontoxic" and "natural" claims are meaningless because unregulated, advises* Consumer Reports **(www.greenerchoices.org).**

LIQUID CO_2

The other dry cleaning alternative listed as environmentally preferable by the EPA, this choice is green and nontoxic because it uses what is known as "food-grade" carbon dioxide, the same gas that makes soda and beer bubbly.

In 2003, *Consumer Reports* tested CO_2-based cleaning systems and found the results to be better than traditional dry cleaning. To locate these services near you, go to www.findCO2.com

Not to be confused with operations such as coal-burning power plants, which release CO_2, the principal global warming gas, CO_2 cleaners actually clean and reuse this naturally occurring substance.

REDUCING PERC

Can't find an alternative cleaner? You can still take these commonsense steps to reduce your exposure to perc.

- Let your laundry "offgass" outside your home. When you tote your clothes back from the cleaner's, remember that perc residue clings to the fabric and fills the plastic bags.

- Debag at the shop, and let the clothes air out on your way home.

- If your cleaning is delivered, remove it from the bags immediately and hang in the porch or entryway, or by an open window.

If you live or work near a dry cleaners, and smell fumes, call your city or state department of health . . . and request an inspection.

Recycling recaptures the heavy

metals in inks, keeping them out of the

waste stream and our water.

Reduce, Reuse, Recycle

10

ONE GREEN THING

Receive and pay bills online rather than using snail mail.

Why? If every U.S. home did this, we'd reduce paper waste by 1.6 billion tons a year and cut greenhouse gases by 2.1 million tons a year.

How can I choose and use paper and wood products in ways that cause the least harm to forests?

Make sure the paper has at least some recycled content, or, in the alternative, that it's not made from trees at all.

GREEN PAPER AND WOOD PRODUCTS

choose it

Use paper and wood products with the following labels:

- Ecologo-certified (www.ecologo.org)

- Forest Stewardship Council (FSC): certified as coming from forests managed to forbid pesticides and restrict cutting of old-growth trees and destruction of ecosystems (www.woodwise.org)

- Green Seal: certifies that natural resources were conserved and toxic waste reduced (www.greenseal.org)

- Post-Consumer-Recycled (PCR)

lose it

Stop using the following:

- Chlorine-bleached paper

- Furniture and paneling made from tropical hardwoods, such as mahogany and teak, which do not have FSC certification

- Virgin paper products

Stop engaging in the following practices:

- Stop catalogs and direct mail from being sent to you (see Take Action, page 234)

- Using only one side of paper

- Buying new wrapping paper

- Tossing recyclable paper in the trash

choose it

- Post-Consumer Waste (PCW)
- Processed Chlorine Free (PCF)
- Recycled/reclaimed "Good Wood": certified by the Rainforest Alliance
- Totally Chlorine Free (TCF)

Use products made from the following alternative materials:

- Bagasse (sugar cane)
- Elephant dung(!)
- Hemp
- Knaff
- Recycled blue jeans

Take the following green steps:

- Print and copy on both sides of paper
- Save and reuse wrapping paper
- Recycle paper

The following is better than virgin, but not ideal:

- "Recycled" paper, which means it's pre-consumer, not post-consumer, taken from factory waste. Not as green, because it's not being reused.

better for your health

The chlorine bleaching of wood pulp to make paper releases cancer-causing dioxins into our air, farm fields, and water. These chemicals rise in the food chain, collecting in animal fats and in our bodies.

Recycling recaptures the heavy metals in inks, keeping them out of the waste stream and our water. Preserving rainforests, the home of the highest number of different species on earth, also preserves natural medicines and potential cures for diseases. Scientists are continually discovering new species of plants and animals in these biodiversity hotspots.

better for the planet

Recycling paper and choosing certified and recycled forest products saves trees and forest ecosystems. According to the EPA, each one of us uses the equivalent of one 100-foot-tall Douglas fir tree in paper and wood products every year. Big, old-growth trees in boreal (northern) and tropical forests keep more carbon out of the atmosphere than younger trees and tree plantations do. Logging releases carbon into the atmosphere and is a principal source of global warming emissions.

Producing junk mail consumes about one hundred million trees and 28 billion gallons of water a year.

Recycling paper produces far fewer greenhouse gases than producing virgin paper. One ream (500 sheets) of 100 percent PCW paper saves 5 pounds of CO_2, according to www.stopglobalwarming.org. Recycling one ton of paper saves 17 mature trees, 7,000 gallons of water, 3 cubic yards of landfill space, 2 barrels of oil, and 4,100 kilowatt hours of electricity, which could power an average home for 5 months, according to the EPA.

At the current rate of 4.6 pounds of solid waste a day, each American generates his/her own weight in garbage a month, according to the Michigan Center for Sustainability Systems. Paper comprises at least 30 percent of landfill waste.

Recycling your household paper, plastic, and glass can reduce the emission of 1,000 pounds of CO_2 a year.

better for the budget

While high-percentage PCW paper is a bit pricier than virgin paper, printing and copying on both sides of the paper saves you a lot.

GOOD NEWS!

People are using 25 percent less paper per person, and paper recycling has grown by 27 percent, according to the 2009 State of Green Business Report (www.greenbiz.com).

RECYCLED OFFICE PAPER

PCW (from 30–100 percent) chlorine-free, eco-certified, and tree-free paper can be found at the following places (buy paper with the highest percentage of PCW available):

www.badgerpaper.com

www.dolphinblue.com

www.greenfieldpaper.com

www.mohawkpaper.com

www.newleafpaper.com

www.recycledproducts.org

www.staples.com

www.thepapermillstore.com

www.treecycle.com

GreenerPenny's
BEST HOUSEHOLD PAPER LIST

Try to use washable cloth kitchen towels, napkins, and hankies as a rule. When only paper will do, the following companies use PCF bleached and 60–80 percent PCW recycled paper in their tissues, paper towels, napkins, and/or toilet paper. It's a shame, but tall virgin trees in northern forests are still being logged for lowly toilet paper!

Atlantic Packaging's "Ambiance," "Atlantic," "Fiesta," and "April Soft" brands (www.atlantic.ca)

Cascade "North River" brand (www.cascades.com)

Earth First (www.safeway.com)

Marcal (www.marcalpaper.com)

Planet (www.planetinc.com)

Seventh Generation (www.seventhgeneration.com)

Whole Food's 365 (www.wholefoodsmarket.com)

RUNNER-UP

Kimberly Clark's Scott paper products: They will now use 40 percent recycled or FSC certified content.

For more information, log on to www.greenerpenny.com.

RECYCLING TIPS

What to Recycle, and How

The easy stuff (most municipalities now pick it up) includes paper, plastics (those with recycling codes #1 or #2), glass, and metal (aluminum cans, stainless steel). For a one-stop place to find out how to recycle almost anything, go to www.earth911.com and type in the name of the item, from old paint to cell phones, and your zip code. Presto! You're one step closer to a pristine planet.

APPLIANCES

Okay, this is a tough one that not even Earth911 can solve yet.

For refrigerators, freezers, and air-conditioners, the Environmental Protection Agency has launched a Responsible Appliance Disposal Program, starting with the take-back of refrigerators, in order to safely capture the chemical coolants known as chlorofluorocarbons (CFCs). CFCs are ozone-layer-destroying chemicals that also contribute to global warming. Sears has committed to taking back one million refrigerators. For more information, see www.epa.gov.

For all appliances, check with your municipal waste department to see if they have a recycling program.

Most appliances contain a lot of steel, the most recyclable metal; search for a facility near you at www.recyclesteel.org.

COMPUTERS

Of course you don't want your old machine to turn up as toxic e-waste in China, India, Ghana, or Pakistan, polluting water and air and exposing unprotected recycling workers to harmful chemicals. But 50–80 percent of discarded computers are shipped overseas, and only 10 percent of U.S. computers are recycled, according to the watchdog nonprofit Silicon Valley Toxics Coalition. Many computer companies, including Apple, Dell, Gateway, Sony, and Toshiba, offer free take-back and recycling programs for their products. If you buy a new Apple or Dell, they'll even recycle your old computer made by another manufacturer. And the Dell Outlet store sells recycled, refurbished, upgraded computers at a lower-than-retail price, extending their lifespan well beyond the average two-year mark.

One way to make sure your computer doesn't pollute impoverished communities abroad is to make sure it stays in this country, being productively used. The National Cristina Foundation is a nonprofit that gives computers to disabled and economically disadvantaged children and adults in all fifty states and Canada. See www.cristina.org.

For more on e-waste, visit Basel Action Network (www.ban.org) and the Silicon Valley Toxics Coalition (www.etoxics.org).

CELL PHONES

If Americans recycled the more than one hundred million cell phones they throw away each year, it would save enough energy to power 18,500 homes, according to the EPA. We'd also keep an annual 65,000 tons of e-waste, some of it highly toxic, out of the environment.

How to recycle a cell phone? Often, it's as simple as dropping your phone off in a bin at the store where you bought it. Or find a drop-off recycling center near you by entering your zip code at www.call2recycle.com.

To hook up with a charity in your area who'll take your used electronics and tech items, including computers, cell phones, printers, and digital cameras, go to www.collectivegood.com/electronics_recycling.asp or www.mygreenelectronics.org. Many Goodwill and Salvation Army thrift stores are also happy to accept working computers and TVs, but call ahead before you drop them off, because some of these secondhand stores won't accept them.

Many college campuses have phone and computer recycling programs.

In early 2009, all Best Buy stores began accepting most electronic products, including phones, computers, and televisions up to 32 inches wide, for recycling.

There is a $10 fee for anything with a screen, but you get a $10 Best Buy gift card when you pay it. See www.bestbuyinc.com/corporate_responsibility/our_planet _recycling.htm.

TELEVISIONS

Because one TV monitor can contain 4–8 pounds of toxic lead, you don't want to risk your old set's spilling its guts in a dump. Check with your municipality's solid waste department about pickup services or drop-off centers for recycling large electronics. Or call around. Best Buy will pick up your old set when it delivers a new one. Office Depot accepts old TVs for recycling. Sony has drop-off centers (www.sony.com/recycle).

Hazardous Waste

The following household hazardous wastes should not go in the regular trash or recycling bins:

Antifreeze

Batteries

Compact fluorescent light (CFLs) bulbs

Paints and solvents

Pesticides

For all of your recycling needs, call your municipal waste department for pickup schedules or drop-off locations, or search at the indispensable www.earth911.com. For more info, see www.epa.gov/epawaste/index.htm.

And don't forget www.freecycle.org and www.craigslist.org, where your still-functioning items can be traded or given away to folks who will gladly take them off your hands, giving them a new and productive home.

III. *Personal Care and Apparel*

. . . balance more affordable, if less

pure products that work for you,

against green cosmetics.

ONE GREEN THING

To reduce risky exposure as much as possible, choose personal care products whose lists of ingredients *do not include* the word *fragrance*.

Why? "Fragrance" generally means synthetic fragrance, and is present in many personal care products, everything ranging from shampoo to sunless tanners, from moisturizer to mascara. The seemingly harmless label often means *that a product contains phthalates or other toxic chemicals.*

I. GENERAL PERSONAL CARE PRODUCTS

Also note that the claim "natural" by itself, without a reliable third-party certifier's seal, is meaningless (see the "Better Beauty Labels" chart on pages 163–165). Even toxins such as the heavy metals lead and mercury are "natural" in origin, after all. So is petroleum, from which toxic synthetic chemicals are made.

While most companies are required by law to list all a product's ingredients on the label, there are exceptions. The stand-alone word *fragrance* permits companies to hide components of synthetic scents behind a catch-all phrase. That's because so-called trade secrets such as fragrance formulas are protected by law.

BALANCING YOUR GREEN COSMETIC BUDGET

No need to stress your budget or change your whole regimen. Instead, balance more affordable, if less pure products that work for you against green cosmetics following the highest standards (and sometimes having the highest prices). A little green goes a long way.

For example, one of my favorites, an eye cream by a leading "natural" cosmetics company, is rated a moderate-hazard "4," on a scale of 1 to 10.

see EWG's
www.cosmeticsdatabase.com.
But I'm not giving it up! So I try to even out my risks by alternating my use of this eye cream with a purer one in my daily regimen.

FRAGRANCE IN PERSONAL CARE PRODUCTS

👍 choose it

When reading labels, look for the following:

Non-synthetic fragrances consisting of plant essential oils, which are listed by their names. Examples: lavender, rose, and other flowers; lemon and other citrus fruits; rosemary and other herbs; vanilla, ginger, and other spices.

Genuinely "unfragranced" products, such as pure shea or cocoa butter, without added fragrant essential oil scents. Read labels and sniff testers.

👎 lose it

Avoid products whose ingredients lists include the following terms:

Fragrance: This is a code word for synthetic fragrance, which can contain phthalates and other chemicals classified as high-risk ingredients on EWG's Skin Deep database (www.safecosmetics.org).

Fragrance-free/Unscented: These terms, for which the FDA has set no guidelines, can mean that fragrances have been added to neutralize other scents, according to Consumers Union's eco-labels project at www.greenerchoices.org.

Hypoallergenic/Sensitivity tested/Non-irritating/Allergy tested/Dermatologist tested: These are all meaningless labels, per the Consumers Union.

Fragrance is the number one ingredient associated with allergic reactions.

Skin and Hair

155

better for your health

You'll protect your hormonal system, and that of your offspring. By side-stepping "fragrance," you reduce exposure to phthalates, a family of hormone-disrupting chemicals found in all of our bodies, but at their highest levels in children and in women of childbearing age.

Phthalates are commonly used to make perfumes last longer and keep nail polish from flaking. The chemicals cross the umbilical cord from mother to fetus, and exposures are thought to be most problematic in the eighth to fifteenth weeks of pregnancy, when a fetus begins to develop as either male or female.

You'll have fewer allergic reactions. Fragrance is the number one ingredient associated with allergic reactions. Allergies can trigger asthma attacks in sensitive people. Any strong fragrance, including natural ones, can provoke irritated eyes and noses, and asthma. To counter this, read ingredients lists and select products that are free of specific plant oils you may be allergic to. Citrus, for example, is a common allergen. You don't have this option with labels that hide perfuming agents behind the word *fragrance*. In addition, natural scents will vanish faster; synthetics are made to be longer lasting, and thus will prolong any allergic reactions.

better for the planet

Developmental changes in wildlife first alerted scientists to the hormone-disrupting properties of chemicals in everyday products that found their way into the environment. Alligators downstream from sewage plants were being born with deformities; panthers were suffering from abnormalities; and bald eagles' egg shells were thinning, harming reproductive rates to the point that the bald eagle became endangered. In 1996, wildlife biologist Theo Colburn, Ph.D., summarized these findings and launched the study of hormone disruption in the book *Our Stolen Future*.

In lab tests, phthalates in synthetic fragrances have been found to alter sexual development and cause cancer in lab animals, which means that wildlife may also be at risk. While plant oils in personal care products biodegrade after they're washed down the drain, phthalates and other synthetic chemicals have been found to mess with normal development in fish and other aquatic life.

Botanical ingredients, unlike chemicals made from petroleum, are renewable, so when we use them we aren't depleting the planet's natural resources. It's even better to choose products listing certified organic plant essential oils, which are cultivated without pesticides, using methods that enrich and preserve the soil.

II. COSMETICS

most-asked question

What are the specific ingredients I should most avoid in cosmetics?

See GreenerPenny's Filthy Fifteen list for fifteen of the most commonly used and problematic ingredients to look out for and avoid if you possibly can.

GreenerPenny's *Filthy Fifteen*
PERSONAL CARE INGREDIENTS TO AVOID

The following list of toxic ingredients was compiled with the help of Olga Naidenko and Sean Gray, senior scientist and senior analyst, respectively, at EWG; Stacy Malkan, author of *Not Just a Pretty Face: The Ugly Side of the Beauty Industry* (New Society, 2007); and the Organic Consumers Association (www.organicconsumers.org).

Using numerical risk ratings from the Environmental Working Group and the Campaign for Safe Cosmetics Skin Deep database (www.cosmeticsdatabase.com), I've indicated moderate-hazard ingredients with one asterisk (*), and moderate-to-high hazard ingredients with two asterisks (**). (Note: Ratings vary according to how chemicals are used, for instance, in shampoo versus makeup.)

1. Aluminum starch/octenylsuccinate**, an anti-caking agent and fragrance found in lipsticks, lotions, sunblocks, eye makeup, powders, and FD&C blue, red, and yellow colors; linked to cancer and developmental/reproductive harm.

2. Antibacterials/antimicrobials such as Triclosan**: found in deodorants, moisturizers, toothpaste, liquid hand soaps, and body wash; suspected of contributing to the spread of antibiotic-resistant bacteria.

3. Coal tar colors**: found in dandruff shampoos, psoriasis and eczema treatments, hair dyes, and makeup; includes FD&C and D&C colors, especially blue 1 and green 3; suspected carcinogenis.

4. Cocamidopropyl betaine*: a sudsing agent; can produce allergic reactions.

5. Ethoxylated chemicals (the "PEGs" and "eths"): sudsing/moisturizing agents made by adding ethylene oxide to fatty acids so they'll become more water soluble; process can create carcinogenic 1,4 dioxane**. Watch out for: PEG-80 sorbitan laurate**, PEG-6 methyl ether*, polyethylene glycol**, PEG-20**, sodium laureth sulfate*, sodium coco sulfate (from coconut)*, ceteareth-20 and -30**, and many more substances with "PEG" and "eth" in their names.

6. Formaldehyde**: preservative and known human carcinogen/allergen used in some nail and hair products, including dyes, and present as a contaminant in nearly all other types of personal care products; look also for diazolidinyl urea, imidazolidinyl urea, and quaternium compounds, which are also strong irritants.

7. Fragrance**: fragrance, which, ironically, can also be added to mask other scents in so-called "fragrance-free" products, is widely found in lipstick, skin lotions; as a catch-all term, it can include phthalates**, isoeugenol**, cinnamal**, and BHT*; all linked to cancer and developmental/reproductive harm, allergies.

8. Heavy metals**: neurotoxins that include lead and mercury; lead** has been found in several brand-name lipsticks, and mercury** can crop up in eye makeup, including kohls and mascaras; can cause nervous system and brain damage.

9. Nano particles*: possible brain damage, cancer risks. (See "Nanotechnology and Personal Care Products" on pages 161–162.)

10. Oxybenzone/benzophenone**: found in sunscreens; risk of cancer, hormone disruption.

11. Petroleum distillates: widely found in mascara, wart removers; suspected carcinogenis.

12. Polyethylene**: a plastic used as a film, binder, or stabilizer in lipsticks, mascaras, and other makeup; it is ethoxylated and may be contaminated with 1,4 dioxane.

13. P-Phenylenediamine (PPD): found in hair dyes and bleaches; possible risk of cancer, developmental/reproductive harm, and allergies.

14. Preservatives: include BHA**, methylparaben**, and other parabens*, which have been found in breast cancer tumors and which stimulate growth of breast cancer cells in the lab.

15. Silica**: anti-caking agent; a risk mostly when used in powders that can be easily inhaled; mica and talc, also used in powders, are less risky, although talc* is listed as a moderate hazard by EWG because it can be contaminated with fibers similar to cancer-causing asbestos.

RUNNERS-UP

Say no to these specialty treatments:

Hydroquinone/Resorcinol: used in acne treatments, skin lighteners, and as a "developer" in hair dyes and bleaches; linked to cancer and allergies.

Salicylic acid: found in acne treatments, dandruff shampoos, moisturizers, astringent/toners, and facial washes; linked to cancer, developmental/reproductive harm.

For more information, log on to www.greenerpenny.com.

NANOTECHNOLOGY AND PERSONAL CARE PRODUCTS

another question

I like the idea of using natural mineral makeup for eye shadows, foundation, powders, and bronzers, but I hear that they sometimes use nanoparticles. What is nanotech, and is it a problem?

You're right to be concerned. Many mineral makeups and sunblocks rely on nanotechnology to give them a smooth texture and transparency. The problem: like little Trojan horses, nanoparticles, which are smaller than a billionth of a meter, have shown an ability to penetrate the skin, entering the bloodstream. A recent study found that toxins and toxic chemicals can "piggyback" on nanoparticles, getting carried deeper into the body. Studies also show that nanoparticles, which are also used as antibacterial "silver" coatings in washing machines and on fabrics, are fast entering the environment and may pose risks to wildlife.

What to do? Choose non-nano makeup, but don't be afraid of mineral sunblocks, Environmental Working Group advises. EWG's reasoning: makeup is a non-essential product, but sunblock is a necessity. EWG recommends choosing mineral sunblock, nano-ized or not, over synthetic sunblocks, which appear to pose greater health risks, based on scientific research to date. Makes sense to me!

How to avoid nano? While there's no requirement that labels disclose nanoparticles, the word *micronized* means that particles are larger than 100 nanometers—a safer size. According to EWG, particles in the 20–60 nanometer range are most easily absorbed by skin or inhaled deep into the lungs. As a general rule, choose opaque, rather than sheer, mineral makeup; the particles, because they're so visible, are likely to be larger than 100 nanometers.

As an alternative to mineral powders, try cornstarch or silk. Look for low-risk makeup powders, eye makeups, bronzers, and blush at www.cosmeticsdatabase.com.

another question

I'm confused by all the new eco-beauty labels. Which labels and claims ensure that a beauty product is free of the most harmful man-made ingredients?

See the "Choose It/Lose It" table, at right, for standards rated with the help of David Bronner, president of Dr. Bronner's Magic Soaps, and Stacy Malkan, of the Campaign for Safe Cosmetics and Health Care Without Harm.

Do One Green Thing

BETTER BEAUTY LABELS

👍 choose it

The following seals ensure that products are free of the most toxic ingredients known. To avoid conflicts of interest, certifiers should be independent from the cosmetics industry. The gold green standard for cosmetics is "USDA Certified Organic."

Australian Certified Organic: uses stringent standards similar to the USDA's; accredited by the International Federation of Organic Agriculture Movements (www.australianorganic.com.au; ifoam.org).

BDIH (Association of German Industries and Trading Firms): very strict natural cosmetics seal prohibiting all petroleum-based ingredients (www.kontrollierte-naturkosmetik.de).

Certified USDA Organic: 95 percent certified organic ingredients.

ECO-CERT: this EU third-party mark specifies 10 percent organic and 95 percent natural ingredients, but does allow some synthetics, so read ingredients lists carefully (www.ecocert.com).

👎 lose it

The following labels and claims are confusing and/or misleading, or have been deemed "meaningless" by the Consumers Union's Greener Choices Eco-label Project and/or by a 2007 survey of "greenwashing" retail claims conducted by Terrachoice, an environmental marketing firm with an Ecologo third-party seal:

Chemical Free/No Chemicals

Contains No Hazardous Ingredients per OSHA Regulations

Earth Smart

Environmentally/Eco Safe

Environmentally Friendly

Natural

Organic: when this appears on the label of a product that is not certified organic or does not contain certified organic ingredients

Be on the lookout also for fair trade claims without certification or substantiation, and for the terms:

Cruelty-free

100% Vegan

100% Vegetarian ingredients

Made with Organic: minimum 70 percent certified organic ingredients; no synthetic preservatives; all major cleansing and moisturizing ingredients are made from organic, not conventional or petroleum-based, products (www.ams.usda.gov/NOP).

NPA (Natural Products Association): their seal, launched in 2008, bars many toxic/irritating ingredients, including phthalates, parabens, and sodium laureth *and* lauryl sulfate.

NSF/ANSI (National Sanitation Foundation International/American Natural Standards Institute): their seal requires the product to be 70 percent organic (using the Quality Assurance Institute, an NOP [National Organic Program] third-party certifier) and strictly minimize use of synthetics (www.nsf.org).

OASIS (Organic and Sustainable Industry Standards): this EU seal specifies 85 percent organic ingredients, but uses industry, not third-party, certifiers (www.oasisseal.org).

The Soil Association: an EU seal from the respected UK organic farming research institute that's not quite as stringent as USDA organic; allows more synthetics (www.soilassociation.org).

Whole Foods Premium Body Care: this green in-store shelf tag flags products that are free of 250 toxic chemicals per Campaign for Safe Cosmetics criteria (www.wholefoodsmarket.com/wholebody/pbc).

Also meaningful are the following labels:

Certified Vegan: no ingredients taken from animals.

Fair Trade Certified: plant ingredients are sourced from cooperatives that ensure living wages, humane working conditions, and other benefits to workers and their families (see www.transfairusa.org, and IMO's Fair for Life, Institute for Marketecology, at www.fairforlife.net).

Leaping Bunny: certified free of animal testing.

The following labels are only somewhat meaningful (Consumers Union reminds us that these claims are not verified by third parties):

No DEA*

No Methyl/Propyl-Paraben*

No Sodium Lauryl/Laureth Sulfate*

No Synthetic Detergents**

*According to CU's www.eco-labels.org, labels that claim products are free of specific chemicals can be relied on. However, similar, un-disclaimed chemicals, such as butyl parabens, may still be there, so look sharp!
**Consumers Union points out that this could apply also to detergents made from natural sources that can have similar ill effects.

NOTE ON "NATURAL"

Always bear in mind that some truly natural substances can be irritating and toxic: think of poison oak and ivy. In 2009, for example, the FDA ordered that carmine/cochineal, a color made from an insect, be spelled out on ingredients lists because it can be highly allergenic.

Skin and Hair

165

III. SKIN CARE

Use products with the simplest ingredients—pure plant oils, minerals—on your skin.

GOOD NEWS!

In response to consumers' very sensible concerns regarding what we put on our skin, which is highly absorptive and the body's largest organ, the market for natural personal care is booming. Beauty products with certified organic ingredients are now sold by major retailers such as Walmart and Target. Sales are growing at the rate of 13 percent a year, far outpacing the general personal care market's 3 percent. Many research firms predict a continued boom in natural cosmetics.

AVOIDING CHEMICAL EXPOSURE FROM PERSONAL CARE PRODUCTS

Did you know that cosmetics and personal care products are the leading reason for calls to poison control centers in the United States?

Only 11 percent of the 10,500 ingredients in personal care products have been safety tested, according to the Campaign for Safe Cosmetics. Many chemicals banned in cosmetics by the European Union haven't even been reviewed by the U.S. Food and Drug Administration, the responsible agency in this country. Some companies actually make one  formulation of, say, a shampoo or mascara for Europe and a different one, with all the toxic ingredients left in, for the United States, as reported by Mark Schapiro in *Exposed* (Chelsea Green, 2007).

Every day, one out of every thirteen U.S. women, and one out of every twenty-

See
www.aapcc.org.

three men, is exposed to cosmetic ingredients that are known or probable human carcinogens, according to the Environmental Working Group. The average woman uses twelve different beauty products daily, and the average teenager uses seventeen. Through our personal care routines alone, not to mention through our food, plastics, and indoor and outdoor air, we are getting multiple doses of the same chemicals, such as phthalates, and a mixture of different chemicals that may have harmful interactions in our bodies.

Meanwhile, you can avoid being an inadvertent guinea pig by choosing products free of GreenerPenny's Filthy Fifteen personal care ingredients (see page 158), and those made by GreenerPenny's Top Natural Cosmetics Companies in the list on pages 176–181).

another question

Shouldn't I also be worried about mineral oil and paraffin?

Don't sweat it. Although mineral oil and paraffin are hydrocarbons, made from petroleum and linked to cancers in some cases, both are listed as low-to-moderate hazards by the Cosmetics Database (www.cosmeticsdatabase.com). Environmental Working Group warns against mineral oil sprays, droplets from which can be inhaled, and paraffin in lip products, which can be ingested.

For a downloadable list of cosmetics ingredients to avoid, see www.greenerpenny.com.

Many cosmetic companies nowadays have a regular and an organic line. Can we assume that their regular lines are greener, too?

No. We can't even assume that their "organic" lines are truly organic if there is no reputable certifier's seal on the packaging (see the "Better Beauty Labels" chart on page 163). In 2008, the Organic Consumers Association and Dr. Bronner's filed suit against several personal care companies on the grounds that their use of the word *organic* was misleading and exposed consumers to hazardous chemicals that had been found in their products by OCA lab tests.

ONE GREEN THING

Use products with the simplest non-synthetic ingredients on your skin.

Why? Synthetic chemicals linked to cancer and hormone disruption are readily absorbed through skin and make their way into our bloodstream.

most-asked question

What ingredients should I most avoid in the products I put on my skin?

Synthetic preservatives, including parabens (prefaced by methyl-, propyl-, ethyl-, and butyl-), which have been found in human breast cancer tumors and have also provoked the growth of human breast cancer cells in lab tests.

INGREDIENTS IN PRODUCTS FOR THE SKIN

choose it

- Plant-derived, essential oil preservatives that inhibit bacteria growth. These include:

    Aloe vera · Citrus seed extract

    Clove oil · Cranberry extract

    Cypress · Eucalyptus · Grapeseed

    Lavender · Neem · Rose

    Rosemary · Sage · Thyme

    Witch hazel

- Plant-derived moisturizing agents:

    Jojoba oil/butter · Olive oil/butter

    Shea oil/butter

lose it

- Synthetic, petroleum-derived preservatives:

    Parabens (methyl-, propyl-, butyl-, ethyl-, isobutyl-) BHA

- Petroleum-derived moisturizing agents that are very allergenic and also linked to cancer); these include:

    Propylene glycol (linked to hormone disruption)

    Phenoxyethanol

- Palm oil: it's natural, but growing it in plantations destroys natural forests

Skin and Hair

169

better for your health

Paraben preservatives promote the growth of breast cancer cells in lab studies and have been found in breast cancer tumors. Several cancer organizations advise that products containing parabens not be applied to the body. In 2004, researchers at the University of Reading, UK, established that parabens collect in human breast tissue, and noted that deodorants might be a route of exposure.

Ranked a ten, or highest hazard, by www.cosmeticsdatabase.com, BHA is linked to cancers, reproductive harm, allergies, and other such major concerns.

better for the planet

BHA persists in the environment rather than breaking down; it collects in water and soil and in living organisms, infecting the food chain.

Sales in natural cosmetics
are growing at the rate of
13 percent a year.

Moisturizers

As someone who's been tormented by oily skin all my life, the last thing I wanted to do was *put* oil on my face! But one summer, at my husband's family's mountain cabin, I learned that dry air can actually crack your face. My sister-in-law persuaded me to try her remedy: pure jojoba oil from the health food store. It makes your skin and hair feel soft, and it's so light it doesn't clog your pores.

OILS

The following oils can be used on facial or body skin and dry hair ends: Kiehl's Superbly Restorative Argan Dry Oil and Jurlique Balancing Rose Oil.

BODY CREAM

For the body, there's Organic Essentials shea butter cream, and L'Occitane bio lavender body cream.

FACE CREAM

For the face, try Dr. Hauschka Rose Day Cream, Wcleda Rose Cream, Pangea Organics Rose Geranium, or Origins organics.

EYE CREAM

Burt's Bees Radiance Royal Eye Jelly is a green alternative to standard under-eye creams.

Safer Sunblocks

most-asked question

What's the most important ingredient to avoid in sunscreen?

Benzophenone (BP-3), also known as oxybenzone.

Why: It's rated a high hazard by Environmental Working Group (www.cosmeticsdatabase.com) and it gets under your skin.

Ninety-seven percent of Americans in a recent study by the U.S. Centers for Disease Control were found to have this common sunscreen ingredient in their bodies. See the chart below for ingredients to choose and to avoid.

ACTIVE INGREDIENTS IN SUNSCREENS/BLOCKS

choose it

These natural minerals are the least toxic and most effective sun barriers. They protect against both UVA and UVB rays.

- Titanium Dioxide
- Zinc Oxide

lose it

These synthetic chemicals can be allergenic and toxic. They may not protect effectively against UVA rays.

- Benzophenone/oxybenzone
- Homosalate
- Octinoxate/Octyl Methoxycinnamate
- Padimate O (PABA)
- Parsol 1789/Avobenzone

Do One Green Thing

172

better for your health

BP-3, also known as oxybenzone, is rated highly hazardous by EWG because it can cause allergic reactions and is a suspected human hormone disruptor. Octinoxate and homosalate, rated moderately hazardous, have also shown the potential to interfere with hormonal systems. Other synthetic sunscreen chemicals, Parsol 1789 and Padimate-O, may cause DNA damage to skin cells when exposed to sunlight.

> Avoid sunblocks in spray form, because the droplets are easily inhaled, carrying any natural toxins or toxic chemicals into the lungs.

better for the planet

In addition, what isn't absorbed by your skin can wash off and hurt aquatic ecosystems: BP-3 and octyl methoxycinnamate have been shown to provoke allergic symptoms in people and contribute to viral infections in coral reefs; BP-3 has been implicated in the feminization of male fish, which start producing eggs.

What to look for:

Happily, there are many effective (SPF 15 and above) mineral sunblocks that are free of such troublesome chemicals. While the minerals may be in nanoparticle form, the skin-saving benefits of sunblocks outweigh the risks—and nano-ized sunblocks may, as a general rule, provide stronger protection than non-nano varieties, EWG says. Still, when given the choice, you may want to opt for non-nano sunblocks, just in case. I do.

In addition, make sure that any sunscreen or block you buy is full-spectrum, which means it keeps out both UVA and UVB rays, and that it has a Sun Protection Factor, or SPF, of at least 15.

BEST GREEN SUNBLOCK SHOPPING LIST

Below is a top tier of sunblocks, chosen because they use only the minerals titanium dioxide and/or zinc oxide as active ingredients, protect against both UVA and UVB rays, and are free of the riskiest synthetic chemicals. As a rule, EWG recommends choosing products with a Sun Protection Factor (SPF) of 30 or higher; however, I have included a couple of pure products with an SPF of 18 that, according to EWG, provide high UVA and medium UVB protection.

Alba Botanical Fragrance Free Mineral Sunscreen SPF 18 (www.albabotanica.com)

Avalon Baby Natural Mineral Sunscreen SPF 18 (www.avalonorganics.com)

Badgerbalm SPF 30 Sunscreen (www.badger.com)

Burt's Bees Chemical-Free Sunscreen (www.burtsbees.com)

California Baby No Fragrance Sunscreen Lotion or Sun Block Stick, both SPF 30 (www.californiababy.com)

Elemental Herbs Kids Natural Broad Spectrum UVA/UVB Sunscreen SPF 20 (www.elementalherbs.com)

Jason Natural or Earth's Best Chemical Free Sun Block (www.drugstore.com)

Lavera Sun Block SPF 40 (www.lavera-usa.com)

Nature's Gate Mineral Sunblock or Sport Block, both SPF 20 (www.naturesgate.com)

Purple Prairie Botanicals Sun Stuff or Sun Stick, both SPF 30 (www.purpleprairie.com)

Soleo Organics Chemical Free Sunscreen SPF 30 (www.amazon.com)

RUNNERS-UP

The following products are mineral-based and free of BP-3, octinoxate and homosalate, but do contain a less-than-ideal ingredient or two.

Aubrey Organics Natural Sun Sunscreens SPF 20-25 (padimate-O) (www.aubreyorganics.com)

Blue Lizard for Face, Baby, or Sensitive Skin SPF 30 (parabens) (www.amazon.com)

Mustela Sun Lotion Bebe SPF 50 (parabens) (www.amazon.com)

Neutrogena Pure & Free Sunblock Stick SPF 60 (www.neutrogena.com)

Clinique City Block SPF 25 (parabens); this convenient tinted cream works as a protective daily makeup, but not for beach wear) (www.clinique.com)

Find out what's in your sunscreen (including whether it's nano or not!) and how it rates for effectiveness at www.ewg.org/cosmetics/report/sun screen09/Beach-Sunscreens. You can also search here for ratings of moisturizers and makeups containing sunscreen.

For more information, log on to www.greenerpenny.com.

TOP NATURAL COSMETIC COMPANIES

TIER 1

The following companies make the best truly natural products, which are, across the board, reliably free of the "Filthy Fifteen" contaminants. (A key for acronyms is located at the end of the chart.)

ALAFFIA: shea butter creams; LB, FT (www.alaffia.com)

AUBREY ORGANICS: shampoos, conditioners, makeup, skin care; CO, NPA, LB, CSC (www.aubrey-organics.com)

BADGER BALM: lip and body balms, creams, and massage oils; all are USDA; they make a safe zinc oxide sun block, too; $ (www.badgerbalm.com)

DR. BRONNER'S: Magic and Sundog soaps, lip balms, shaving cream, shampoos, conditioners; USDA, LB, FT, WFWB, $ (www.drbronners.com)

DR. HAUSCHKA: shampoos, conditioners, makeup, skin care; BDIH (www.drhauschka.com)

DROPWISE ESSENTIALS: lotions, oils; CO by QAI (USDA's international certifier) (www.dropwise.com)

EARTH'S BEAUTY: mineral eye and skin makeup, lip and cheek glaze; CSC, LB (www.earthsbeauty.com)

ECCO BELLA: body and skin care, makeup; CO; complete list of ingredients on website (www.eccobella.com)

FARMAESTHETICS: bath and skin care for women, children, and men; discloses all ingredients in refreshingly short lists (www.farmaesthetics.com)

GABRIEL COSMETICS: lipsticks; LB, CSC (www.gabrielcosmeticsinc.com)

GIOVANNI: hair care, mostly plant-based; $, LB, CO by QAI, others

HAWAIIAN BODY PRODUCTS: tropical lotions, bath salts, lip balms (www.hawaiianbodyproducts.com)

HEALING ANTHROPOLOGY: skin and body care; discloses all ingredients on its website (www.healinganthropology.com)

HONEYBEE GARDENS: skin care, lip and eye makeup, aftershave; CSC (www.honeybeegardens.com)

IKOVE: bath, skin, and hair care; WFWB (www.ikove.com)

JANE IREDALE: mineral makeup, eye shadow, powder (www.janeiredale.com)

JOHN MASTERS ORGANIC: soap, shampoo, hair care; CO (www.johnmasters.com)

J. R. LIGGETT'S SHAMPOO BAR: $ (www.jrliggett.com)

JUICE ORGANICS: skin, hair, and lip care; some with 70 percent CO (www.juiceorganics.com)

KAREN'S BOTANICALS: skin care, cleansers, aromatherapy (www.karensbotanicals.com)

KATHY'S FAMILY: skin care, lotions (www.kathysfamily.com)

KELPHEAD: lotion comes in stroke-on bars (www.kelphead.com)

KIMBERLY SAYER: spa treatments, body and skin care, mud masks (www.kimberlysayer.com)

LAVERA: skin and hair care; BDIH, CSC (www.lavera.com)

LOGONA: skin care, lip and eye makeup; BDIH, CSC (www.naturaleurope.com)

MIESSENCE: shampoo, skin and hair care; CO (www.mionegroup.com)

MOONVALLEY: soothing and healing balms, lotions (www.moonvalleyhoney.com)

NEAL'S YARD: plant-based shaving soaps, hand lotions, shampoos; tells you the exact certified organic percentage (from 1 to 97 percent); CO (www.nealsyardremedies.com)

NVEY ECO: lipsticks; USDA (www.nveymakeup.com)

ORGANIC ESSENCE: all USDA lip balms, creams, and soaps; R, PCR, FSC, C (www.orgess.com)

ORIGINS ORGANICS: nearly all the products in this skin care line, including a deodorant, are USDA Certified Organic; the others have at least 87 percent CO content; R, PCR, FSC (www.origins.com)

PANGEA ORGANICS: skin care; $, CO, R, C (www.pangeaorganics.com)

PERFECT ORGANICS: lip and cheek colors, shea butters; CSC; although there's no third-party certification of the organic claim, all ingredients are plant-based (www.perfectorganics.com)

PLANET BOTANICALS: skin care; CO, E (www.planetbotanicals.com)

RAWGANIQUE: hemp shampoo bar; $, CO (www.rawganique.com)

SENSIBILITY SOAPS: face and body wash, moisturizers, deodorants; Nourish line is USDA (www.sensibilitysoaps.com)

SKYE BOTANICALS: skin care and soaps; CO, WFWB (www.skyebotanicals.com)

TERRESSENTIALS: shampoos and face and body lotions come in either flower essences or fragrance free; $, CO (www.terressentials.com)

TOM'S OF MAINE: toothpaste, soap, deodorant, mouthwash; lists all ingredients (www.tomsofmaine.com)

WELEDA: skin care, deodorant, toothpaste, baby soap, and lotions; NPA, BDIH, WFWB (www.usa.weleda.com)

Companies/brands whose product greenness varies. Some of these companies would be in the first tier if they disclosed all ingredients instead of merely using the term *fragrance*. Some of their products are third-party certified organic or natural. But others may still contain ingredients of concern.

ALMAY PURE BLENDS: eye shadow, blush; $ (www.almaypureblends.com)

AVALON ORGANICS BOTANICALS: hand and body lotion, face creams; $, CSC, some USDA Organic (www.avalonorganics.com)

AVEDA: perfumes, "pure-fumes" essential oils, and lip balms are all plant-based; leader in use of R, PCR, FSC in all their packaging (www.aveda.com)

BEE-CEUTICALS ORGANICS: shampoos; some CO, FT (www.beeceuticals.com)

BODY SHOP: hair and skin care, makeup, men's care; wide variety of natural essential oils, but also lists *fragrance*; sources with in-house Community Trade fair trade program (www.thebodyshop-usa.com)

BURT'S BEES: skin and hair care, makeup, men's care, deodorants; website discloses all ingredients, but a few labels still say *fragrance*, without listing specific components; company reps assure me that Burt's products are phthalate-free, and I believe them, but I also believe in full transparency; $, NPA,CSC, WFWB, R, PCR (www.burtsbees.com)

CALIFORNIA BABY: shampoo, soap, lotions, sunblock; CSC (www.californiababy.com)

CAROL'S DAUGHTER: hair, soap, skin care; says no phthalates (except in their perfume sprays), parabens, etc. (www.carolsdaughter.com)

CLEANWELL: triclosan-free liquid soaps, cleansing wipes (www.cleanwelltoday.com)

DEPTH: seaweed extracts in shampoos, shaving, soap items; CO, WFWB (www.depthbody.com)

Skin and Hair

179

ECO LIPS: pure and simple lip balms use CO, WFWB, but SPF face and lipsticks have benzophenone; $ (www.ecolips.com)

EO: bath, body, skin care, lip balm, shaving products; CO, WFWB (www.eoproducts.com)

HUGO NATURALS: soap, skin care; WFWB (www.hugonaturals.com)

JASON NATURAL ORGANICS AND EARTH'S BEST: organic sunblock (no benzophenone); skin, bath, and hair care, sunblock, men's shaving products, deodorants; some are "made with organic"; 70 percent CO (www.jason-natural.com and www.earthsbest.com)

JR WATKINS NATURAL APOTHECARY: hand and foot lotions, lip balms; NPA (www.jrwatkins.com)

JURLIQUE: lovely botanical face, body, hair, and baby products with no phthalates or parabens, but some shampoos have sodium laureth sulfate and cocamidopropyl betaine; Skin Balancing Face Oil is very pure; all ingredients posted on website (www.jurlique.com)

KIEHL'S: Aloe Vera Biodegradable Liquid Body Cleanser, the first beauty product to be certified ubergreen by Cradle to Cradle, the McDonough/Braungart partnership that weighs the full lifecycle of products. (Hopefully there'll be many more to follow!) In 100 percent PCR bottle; website shows all ingredients of all products (www.kiehls.com)

KISS MY FACE: Obsessively Organic skin and hair care; $, CO (www.kissmyface.com)

L'OCCITANE: their body lotion with CO lavender uses only plant essential oils for fragrance; their shea butter tubs and lip balms are paraben-free; some ingredients are sourced from women's co-ops (www.loccitane.com)

NATURE'S BABY ORGANICS: shampoos, soaps, skin care; CO, WFWB (www.naturesbabyproducts.com)

NATURE'S GATE ORGANICS: reveals all ingredients on their website;

high percentage of plant oils CO by QAI and Ecocert; claims to use no phthalates or parabens, but some of their shampoos, conditioners, and lotions do contain some ethoxylated chemicals, quaternium compounds, and "fragrance" (www.natures-gate.com)

ORGANIC APOTEKE: claim their products are free of phthalates, parabens, ethoxylated chemicals; products are not certified organic; WFWB (www.organicapoteke.com)

ORIGINS: claims it has reformulated *all* its products, organic and regular, to be free of parabens (www.origins.com)

PHYSICIANS FORMULA: Organic Wear eye shadow, powders, blush; $, E (www.physicansformula.com)

STELLA MCCARTNEY: CARE billed as 100 percent organic, but is actually E (www.sephora.com)

SUKI: skin care, lip and cheek colors, creams; LB, CSC; lists all ingredients, but not specific essential oils in "aromas" (fragrance); packaged in glass (www.sukipure.com)

TERRE D'OC: face, bath, and body care based on fairly traded argan, pomegranate, coconut, shea oils; E (www.terredoc.com)

WHOLE FOODS: 365 Everyday Value skin and hair care; $ (www.wholefoodsmarket.com)

YES TO CARROTS: although billed as organic, only their lip balm is USDA; NPA, CO, $ (www.yes-to-carrots.com)

ZINC OXIDE OINTMENT: $ (at drugstores or www.amazon.com)

$ = more affordable • ACO = Australian Certified Organic • BDIH — certified natural • C = some compostable non-plastic packaging • CO = the product contains some certified organic plant ingredients CSC = the company has signed the Compact for Safe Cosmetics pledge to remove toxic ingredients E = ecocert certified • FSC = Forest Stewardship Council–certified forest products • FT = some certified fair trade ingredients • LB = Leaping Bunny–certified cruelty-free • NPA = certified natural • R and PCR = packaging uses recycled or post-consumer-recycled content • USDA = the whole product is USDA Certified Organic • WFWB = some products are Whole Foods Whole Body Premium tagged • Note: for definitions, see the Better Beauty Labels chart on page 163. Kudos to companies for providing full transparency by listing all ingredients, not just the "good" ones, on their websites, to save us from spending hours reading small print in store aisles

For more information, log on to www.greenerpenny.com.

Deodorants

No need to nuke delicate underarm skin. Routine washing with regular soap, which gives pathogens the slip, blotting wetness, and dabbing on a little non-talc powder (see DIY on page 183) should discourage smelly bacteria and help keep things pretty fresh.

Because the underarm is close to the breast, the estrogen-like behavior of some conventional ingredients in deodorants has given rise to concern. Parabens (see pages 164–165) have caused growth of breast cancer cells in lab tests. Aluminum-based compounds, the active ingredients in antiperspirants, temporarily block wetness by clogging sweat ducts. That said, no studies link deodorants or antiperspirants to higher risk of breast cancer in humans, but there are products available that don't contain irritating and potentially hazardous chemicals.

. . . there are products available and potentially

BEST DEODORANT PICKS

Many conventional deodorants are now free of parabens at least. Just check the ingredients list. The following companies' third-party-certified organic or natural deodorants are better for the environment, free of potentially harmful chemicals, and free from "fragrance." (See page 153.)

Burt's Bees

Dr. Hauschka

Logona: Free Spray

Miessence: roll-on

Nature's Gate: Asian Pear and Red Tea

Terressentials

Weleda

Or try this quick DIY: Mix a little baking soda (natural deodorizer) and some cornstarch (to absorb moisture) and pat it on.

For more information, log on to www.greenerpenny.com.

that don't contain irritating hazardous chemicals.

Skin and Hair

IV. SOAP AND SHAMPOO

most-asked question

What should I especially look out for in liquid soaps, bubble baths, and shampoos?

1,4 dioxane and triclosan. In California, 1,4 dioxane is classified as a carcinogen; triclosan, a popular antibacterial, can cause irritation and gastrointestinal upset, harms wildlife, and contributes to antibiotic resistance in bacteria.

SUDSING/SURFACTANT INGREDIENTS IN LIQUID SOAPS AND SHAMPOOS

👍 *choose it*

Sudsing ingredients/processes that don't contain/involve 1,4 dioxane:

Plain soap and warm water

Plant essential oils that inhibit bacteria

👎 *lose it*

Sudsing ingredients contaminated with 1,4 dioxane (see "Filthy Fifteen: Personal Care Ingredients to Avoid," page 158):

Triclosan

better for your health

The American Medical Association and the U.S. Centers for Disease Control advise against regular hand washing with antibacterial/antimicrobial soaps containing triclosan, because it may contribute to the spread of antibiotic-resistant bacteria. Plus, they say, it's no more effective at getting rid of germs than plain soap and warm water.

Triclosan can cause nausea and vomiting; not a good choice in kids' fruit-flavored bubble baths! The U.S. Geological Survey has found triclosan, among other chemicals, in U.S. waterways, threatening our drinking water.

better for the planet

The production of triclosan releases dioxins into the environment, which can cause cancer and infertility in humans and wildlife.

another question

What's safer and greener? Bar soap or liquid soap?

Choose bar soap. On average, it's got fewer ingredients, thus fewer chemicals, and uses less packaging. Many liquid soaps are spiked with antibacterial triclosan, which promotes the spread of antibiotic-resistant bacteria.

Skin and Hair

better for your health

The Environmental Working Group's Skin Deep Database rates both bar soaps and liquid soaps for safety. As many as 160 bar soaps currently on the market are rated "low hazard" (score of zero), versus only 25 liquid hand soaps.

The World Health Organization and the American Medical Association both discourage routine use of antibacterial soap containing triclosan.

better for the planet

Bar soap is minimally packaged, often in recycled materials or materials that are easily recycled. Liquid soaps are packaged mostly in plastic bottles (see page 10 for more on why it is important to avoid plastic bottles).

FEMININE HYGIENE PRODUCTS

Disposable

As with paper, one way you can make a healthy difference for the planet is to buy non-chlorine-bleached tampons and sanitary napkins. Manufacturers include: Natracare (www.natracare.com), which uses organic cotton, and Seventh Generation (www.seventhgeneration.com).

Reusable

Reusable accessories reduce paper in the waste stream. Lunapads makes organic cotton washable menstrual pads and "period panties" (www.lunapads.com), and reusable menstrual cups, made of natural gum rubber or silicone (like some baby bottle nipples), are sold at www.keeper.com.

If every American chose one organic

instead of a non-organic cotton T-shirt,

we'd keep 250,000 tons of chemicals

out of our air, water, and soil.

Clothing

12

ONE GREEN THING

Buy less new clothing, and when you do, ask if you can see it in green—that is, made with sustainably produced or recycled fibers.

Why? Sustainable agriculture is cleaner. Cotton, the most popular natural fiber, is the third most pesticide-doused crop in the United States (after corn and soy). A certified organic cotton T-shirt, on the other hand, is grown free of the one-third pound of agricultural chemicals expended on each regular T-shirt.

Making polyester from recycled clothing, as Patagonia does in its take-back/reuse program, reduces the energy consumed by 76 percent and reduces the greenhouse gases released in making new polyester by 71 percent.

Keep in mind that it's always worth asking a store if they sell products with sustainable materials. Even if a store doesn't currently offer them, your question may help spur them to do so. You can help retailers find green suppliers by referring them to the Green Clothing Manufacturers list on page 202.

If every American chose one organic instead of a non-organic cotton T-shirt, we'd keep 250,000 tons of chemicals out of our air, water, and soil.

most-asked question

I try to buy jeans and sweats, as well as the occasional couture find, at thrift and vintage stores. But I draw the line at underwear! What's the greenest fabric if you're buying new?

Reusing is the greenest apparel choice, and every time we buy an item of secondhand clothing, rather than new, we save the equivalent of a half gallon of gasoline.

   When you do buy new clothes, you have several green fabric options.

GREEN CLOTHING

👍 *choose it*

Here are the greenest clothing fiber choices, followed by the next greenest and runners-up:

GREENEST

Certified organic cotton

Recycled cotton

Recycled polyester, made from used garments

Recycled polyester, made from recycled beverage bottles, including Ecospun fleece

Recycled wool

👎 *lose it*

Here are the least green clothing fiber choices:

Acrylic: made from petroleum

Conventional cotton: grown with toxic synthetic pesticides and fertilizers made from fossil fuels

Conventional silk: cruelty issues arise from the killing of pupae in their cocoons by baking or drowning; not to mention silkworms being fed steroids to produce more!

Clothing

Certified Organic (USDA, O-wool) and Pure Grow/Eco/Greenspun wool forbid dipping sheep in pesticides, and require sustainable grazing practices.

Hemp: a hardy crop, traditionally grown without pesticides or intensive irrigation; better still: certified organic hemp (because it's not grown in the U.S., look for IFOAM or QAI international organic certifier labels)

Linen: made from flax, or linseed, a plant traditionally grown without pesticides or fertilizers; organic flax is also available

Ahimsa/peace silk: pupae are allowed to emerge naturally before cocoons are harvested

NEXT GREENEST

Bamboo: a tough wild grass that grows without pesticides or irrigation; makes a soft, supple fiber

Ingeo: a new synthetic made from corn; greener than petroleum-derived polyester; on the minus side, corn is sprayed with the most pesticides of any U.S. crop

Lyocel (Tencel): although made from wood pulp like rayon, it's greener because 99 percent of the processing chemicals are captured and reused instead of released into the environment

Soy: silky soy fiber is made from the leftovers of manufacturing tofu and soy milk; on the minus side, soybean cultivation uses even more pesticides than cotton does

New polyester: made from petroleum, a nonrenewable resource

Nylon: made from petroleum

PVC (polyvinyl chloride, vinyl): its manufacture from petroleum and chlorine releases cancer-causing dioxins that get into our food

Rayon (viscose, acetate): made from wood pulp, so there are deforestation issues; its processing releases harmful pollutants

theScience

better for your health

Organic cotton: Conventional cotton, corn, and soy pesticides and fertilizers contaminate our drinking water and soil, and drift through the air, leaving residue on other food crops. Organic cultivation doesn't use these chemicals.

better for the planet

Pesticides cause deformities and periodic, massive die-offs among birds, fish, and amphibians.

In general, producing cotton or wool uses only a third as much energy as producing synthetic fibers such as polyester. Avoid new, conventional cotton, though. Because of the copious amounts of fossil-fuel-based chemicals and water used to grow it, conventional cotton has a bigger, more damaging *overall* eco footprint than polyester, organic cotton, or hemp.

Polyester has the biggest energy and greenhouse gas footprint.

COMPARING FABRICS

Polyester

Compared with cotton and hemp, polyester has the biggest energy and greenhouse gas footprint by far. Polyester production uses six times more energy than the growing and spinning of hemp fiber, and ten times more energy than the growing and spinning of organic cotton fiber. Polyester manufacture releases four times more CO_2 than the growing and spinning of organic U.S. cotton.

Hemp

Hemp is naturally pest-resistant, and uses only one third the water that cotton does.

Conventional Cotton

The third most pesticide-intensive crop in the U.S., it's also very thirsty. Taking into account the water used to irrigate the crop and process and dye the fiber, making one pair of cotton stonewashed jeans takes 500 gallons of water. The Aral Sea in Turkey has been drained nearly dry to irrigate cotton fields.

Organic Cotton

Uses the least energy, thanks to savings by not using fossil-fuel derived pesticides and fertilizers.

Recycled Cotton

Recycling cotton saves 20,000 liters of water per kilogram of fiber, so if you can find hip blue jeans at the secondhand shop, grab 'em! Instead of a vintage look made with more polluting chemicals, you'll have the real thing. In addition, some manufacturers (see the list on page 202) use recycled cotton to make new clothes.

Recycled Wool

Recycled wool consumes only half as much energy as new wool. In addition, the standards for certified organic, Pure Grow, Eco-, and Greenspun wool prohibit pesticide dipping, overgrazing, and overcrowding of sheep.

Bamboo

Because it's a fast-growing and renewable grass, bamboo is eco-sounder than fibers made from trees. However, because most bamboo comes from China, where eco standards are less rigorously enforced, there's a chance that forests and other natural ecosystems may be being supplanted by bamboo plantations. Still, while not as eco-friendly as organic cotton or hemp, bamboo is greener than rayon, with a similar smooth feel.

For more information on green choices in clothing, see "Good Stuff" clothing at **www.worldwatch.org/node/1485.**

FABRIC FINISHES AND DYES

most-asked question

Does my conventional cotton T-shirt contain pesticides that can rub off on my skin?

Not unless it's moth-proofed. Pesticide residues are removed from cotton and other fiber crops during the course of cleaning and processing. But fabric treatments can expose you to some iffy chemicals. Some dyes and finishes can irritate skin and release toxic fumes.

SAFER FABRICS

choose it

Untreated or minimally treated fabrics: Simplest is best. Patagonia assures that its organic cotton clothing is untreated.

Wool or snug-fitting cotton pajamas (knit leggings and fitted tops): Both meet the U.S. Consumer Products Safety Commission's fire-resistance requirements.

Unbleached or non-chlorine-bleached clothing.

Pure Grow/Eco/Greenspun wool: It's processed without heavy metals and other water-contaminating toxic chemicals, and untreated by shrink- or moth-proofing.

lose it

The following fabric treatments and "-proofing" chemicals can release formaldehyde or perfluorochemicals, both of which are linked to nervous system harm:

Wrinkle proofing/permanent press

Stain proofing

Water proofing

Moth proofing

Chemical fire retardants (fire resistance is required by law for infants'/children's sleepwear)

COLORS

Cotton that naturally grows in colors: Labels include Colorgrown, Foxfibre, and Colorganic.

Fabrics made with OEKO-TEX certified dyes: No heavy metals used; higher absorption rates result in less runoff in water and less need for alkaline and salt used as fixatives.

Fabrics made with fiber-reactive dyes: These bond to the fiber, releasing less dye in waste-water.

Clothes colored with cold pad batch dyeing processes: They use less energy, water, and chemicals.

Clothes colored with SKAL-certified botanical and natural dyes: These are made according to UK Soil Association organic processing standards.

LESS GREEN

Non-certified "natural," "vegetable," or "low-impact" dyes: The claims aren't regulated; while it's a plus if these dyes aren't made from petroleum, they may still contain heavy metals in the dye fixing agent, or mordant.

Chlorine-bleached

Heavy-metal dyes such as chromium;

Synthetic chemical dyes

better for your health

Synthetic fabric treatments and finishes such as "permanent press," "water/stain repellant," and "flame retardant" can contain formaldehyde, which readily "offgases" (evaporates out of materials), can irritate eyes, nose, and throat, and is classified as a probable human carcinogen by the U.S. Environmental Protection Agency. In addition, these finishes make fabrics less breathable and can provoke overheating and rashes.

Water and stain repellants such as Gore-Tex and Teflon coatings contain per-fluorochemicals (PFCs), which have been found in the blood of 96 percent of children tested by the Centers for Disease Control. They are also found in drinking water. PFCs, including the "Teflon chemical" PFOA, have been linked to cancer, developmental harm, and other issues.

better for the planet

Chlorine bleach, moth-proofing pesticides, heavy-metal dyes, and fixatives run off during fabric processing and contaminate waterways, harming aquatic life and habitat.

Every time we buy an item of new, we save the equivalent

BACK TO THE SOURCE: TRACING YOUR JEANS

Following the food trend, garment companies are putting us in touch with the farmers who grow fibers. When customers buy certified organic clothing made by GreenSource at Walmart, Kmart, and other stores, it comes with a tag that allows them to trace it back to the farmer and through the manufacturing and distribution process.

Patagonia's Footprint Chronicles have slide shows that take you to the Mongolian cashmere goat or New Zealand merino sheep ranch where the materials for your clothing originated.

secondhand clothing, rather than of a half gallon of gasoline.

FAIRLY TRADED APPAREL

Over the past decade, green non-profit organizations such as Rainforest Alliance and Conservation International have begun to include worker and community welfare as well as environmental impacts in their product rating standards. Consumers can also provide support by choosing fairly traded apparel, made by fairly paid workers in factories monitored for safe, humane working conditions—ideally, by independent third parties rather than garment industry representatives or the companies themselves. Below are some labels to look for, from best on down.

UNION MADE: This label means that workers who make the apparel are free to exercise collective bargaining rights seeking better wages and conditions. For lists of companies, see www.coopamerica.org/programs/sweatshops/sweatfreeproducts.cfm.

FAIR TRADE FEDERATION: This organization partners with the Fairtrade Labelling Organization International, a network of independent third-party certifiers, see www.fairtradefederation.org. To find FTF-certified apparel and food companies, go to Global Exchange's website, www.store.gxonlinestore.org.

FAIR TRADE MARK: This seal is administered by the Fair Trade Foundation, which monitors workplaces using independent third parties; see www.fair trade.net/the_fairtrade_mark.html.

GREEN AMERICA APPROVED: Companies displaying this seal have met the socially responsible, fair trade or green standards set by Green America, formerly Co-Op America; see www.coopamerica.org/greenbusiness/sealofap proval.cfm.

FAIR LABOR ASSOCIATION: A non-profit association whose membership includes colleges and apparel companies (such as Adidas, Eddie Bauer, Nike, and Patagonia). FLA allows member companies to do some of their own monitoring, but also verifies their findings using independent third parties; see www.fairlabor.org.

RECYCLE APPAREL

- Donate it to a charity, such as the Salvation Army or Goodwill, and get a tax break, or sell it at consignment/vintage stores.

- Buy recyclable Patagonia poly fleece, organic cotton, and cotton/poly-blended apparel bearing the Common Threads tag.

BUYING RECYCLED FASHIONS

- eko*logic: handmade recycled wool clothing; website offers directory of retail outlets (www.ekologic.com).

- Goodwill stores have recently experienced a surge in popularity and, while they're more actively promoting their secondhand designer clothes, you can still find tres chic bargains. Also browse your local Salvation Army and church/school thrift shops for treasures.

- On & On Clothing: designer fashions made from recycled clothing (www.onandon.ca).

- Preloved's fresh, crisp-looking styles for women and men combine recycled and new materials; their Handcut line is made from 100 percent vintage fabrics (www.preloved.ca/english).

WHERE TO FIND "IT" IN GREEN

Mom always said to buy quality, even if you spend a little more. In fashion, green is firmly established as the new black, and *e*-quality is where it's at.

Green Clothing Companies

AMERICAN APPAREL: basics "Made in the USA"; sustainable edition is organic cotton (www.americanapparel.net)

ANNIE GREENABELLE: this fetching London label uses some organic, recycled and fairly traded fibers (www.equaclothing.com)

ASCENSION: first certified carbon-neutral clothing manufacture (certified by the UK's Carbon Trust); their 100 percent organic cotton T-shirts and hooded sweatshirts are made in a solar-powered Fair Wear Foundation–monitored factory in India; jeans are made of organic cotton and Fair Trade denim; the company states it uses environmentally gentler dyes (www.ascensioncloth ing.co.uk/)

BAABAAZUZU: small Michigan company that makes clothing for kids and adults from recycled wool (www.baabaazuzu.com)

BAMBOOSA: sweatshop-free clothing made of certified organic bamboo fiber blended with organic cotton (www.bamboosa.com)

BANANA REPUBLIC: their Eco-blends include hemp and other lower-impact fibers (www.bananarepublic.com)

BLUE CANOE: organic cotton underwear and clothing for women (www.blue canoe.com)

CIEL: this UK designer uses some chemical-free dyes and recycled fibers, and works with factories that follow fair labor laws (www.ciel.ltd.uk)

COLORGROWN: undyed, naturally green, terracotta, and beige newborn items; bunting gowns, blankets, hats (www.colorgrown.com)

COOLNOTCRUEL: sweat-free wares in organic cotton, alpaca, wool, hemp, and more (www.coolnotcruel.com)

ECOLUTION: hemp clothing, accessories (www.ecolution.com)

EDUN: fairly traded and organic sportswear line created by Ali Hewson and Bono with New York designer Rogan Gregory (www.edun.ie)

EKO*LOGIC: handmade recycled wool clothing (www.ekologic.com)

EILEEN FISHER: includes elegant, easy organic cotton and recycled poly pieces (www.eileenfisher.com)

EMPORIO ARMANI: sometimes offers organic knitwear and cotton/hemp jeans (www.emporioarmani.com)

HEMP SISTERS: groovy duds for the whole family (www.hemp-sisters.com)

INDIGENOUS DESIGNS: organic cotton, organic alpaca, and organic sheep's wool knits made by cooperatives (www.indigenousdesigns.com)

HESS NATUR: organic cotton raincoats waterproofed with beeswax and plant oils (us.hess-natur.com)

KAHALA: a classic Hawaiian wear company has some 100 percent organic cotton aloha shirts (www.kahala.com)

LEVI STRAUS: its Eco line includes great-fitting organic cotton jeans (www.levistraus.com)

LL BEAN is going green with some recycled polyester items, including a PVC-free backpack (www.llbean.com)

LINDA LOUDERMILK: handmade clothing in vintage lace, organic cotton, wool, silk (www.lindaloudermilk.com)

LOOMSTATE: urban organic cotton jeans and T-shirts (www.loomstate.org)

LOYALE makes bikinis and bigger things with 100 percent organic cotton, (www.loyaleclothing.com)

MAGGIE'S FUNCTIONAL ORGANICS/CLEAN CLOTHES: organic cotton, organic wool, organic linen, and pesticide-free hemp clothing (www.organicclothes.com)

PATAGONIA: all cotton sportswear is 100 percent organic and untreated; synchilla fleece is made of recycled soda bottles (www.patagonia.com)

STELLA MCCARTNEY can be counted on for something organic in each collection (www.stellamccartney.com)

THE ORGANIK'S EARTH COLLECTION: includes a burlap bag made in the U.S. from recycled Kona coffee sack, with white recycled sail rope handles (www.theorganik.com).

SWEETGRASS NATURAL FIBERS: simply cut, classy organic cotton and hemp clothing for men and women (www.sweetgrassfibers.com)

WILDLIFE WORKS: organic cotton, hemp, and recycled organic cotton fleece; profits fund community development and wildlife conservation efforts in Kenya (www.wildlifeworks.com)

Note: To see the latest apparel in sustainable materials from the like of Bottega Veneta, Donna Karan, Calvin Klein, Rodarte, and new designers, see Future Fashion at www.Earthpledge.org.

Retailers

A HAPPY PLANET: organic cotton and hemp clothing and goods, including reasonably priced organic cotton undies for women and men (nice boxers!) (www.ahappyplanet.com)

BARNEYS NEW YORK is the place to look for new designer eco fashions from Rogan Gregory, Yves St. Laurent, Philip Lim, John Patrick and those we haven't heard of yet (www.barneys.com)

BEKLINA: hip, fanciful urban chic (www.beklina.com)

ETSY: handmade clothes in greener fabrics, such as Regeneration's blends of organic cotton and soy; vintage clothes and craft supplies are sold by individuals and small producers on this lovely community site (www.etsy.com)

GAIAM: offers Organix, their own line of organic cotton clothing (www.gaiam.com)

GLOBAL EXCHANGE STORE: Fair Trade clothing from around the world (www.store.globalexchange.org)

GREEN LOOP: organic, hemp, linen, and recycled made goods by more than twenty-five eco-conscious designers (www.greenloop.com)

KAIGHT: Lower Manhattan green boutique sensibility (www.kaight.com)

NATURAL CLOTHING COMPANY: fashions for men, women, and children, and sleek organic undies! (www.naturalclothingcompany.com)

NO SWEAT: union-made, sweatshop-free clothing and accessories, plus organic cotton T-shirts made in Jerusalem and the West Bank (www.nosweatapparel.com)

OMALA: bamboo yoga wear and undies (www.omala.com)

RAWGANIQUE: sweatshop-free great women's organic cotton or hemp briefs, camis, and bras, men's boxers, and other clothing (www.rawganique.com; 1-877-729-4367)

TARGET: it's worth keeping an eye out for organic cotton lines made exclusively for them by green designers like Rogan Gregory (www.target.com)

THIRTEEN MILE LAMB AND WOOL COMPANY: certified organic wool clothing, yarn, and fleece (www.lambandwool.com)

UNDER THE CANOPY: no-fuss, soft clothing in a variety of eco-fabrics (eco-fleece, organic cotton, hemp, blends) for men, women, and children (www.underthecanopy.com)

URBAN OUTFITTERS: frequently presents sweet and streetwise garments made of organic cotton and recycled fabric (www.urbanoutfitters.com)

Companies Specializing in Baby Apparel

BABY'S ENCHANTED GARDEN: clothing for infants made from organic cotton and Ecospun, a fabric made from post-consumer soda bottles; maternity intimates also available (www.babysenchantedgarden.com; 1-866-802-2229)

CRYSTAL BABY ORGANICS: organic cotton and organic wool baby clothing and accessories (www.crystalbabyorganics.com)

ECOBABY ORGANICS: organic cotton baby clothes and diapers (www.eco baby.com; 1-888-ECOBABY)

GARDEN KIDS: organic cotton children's clothing, newborn through size eight (www.gardenkids.com)

GREEN BABIES: organic cotton baby clothes (www.greenbabies.com)

KID BEAN: baby clothing and accessories made from organic cotton, hemp, and fleece made from recycled soda bottles (www.store.kidbean.com; 1-954-942-2830)

NUI ORGANICS: organic wool baby clothes and accessories; online store (www.nuiorganics.com; 1-888-823-6480)

CLOTH DIAPERS AND COVERS: A CONVENIENT TRUTH

most-asked questions

Which are better for the environment, reusable or disposable diapers?

It's a tossup. Although washing cloth diapers in hot water consumes energy, disposable diapers clog landfills. Better to ask what's more convenient—and economical? I say, both. When at home, if you have a laundry machine (and, ideally, outdoor space to line-dry, as sunlight is a great sterilizer), use cloth. When you're out and about, or traveling, use disposables without guilt.

Which are better for your budget?

Affordability became a new element in the diaper debate for parents during the recent recession, and many found that reusable cloth diapers were more economical.

THE HYBRID DIAPER

The G diaper is partly washable, partly disposable, with a flushable absorbent pad. Uses absorbent gel. Certified C2C (www.gdiaper.com).

Clothing

Baby Needs

The companies listed here sell organic cotton, hemp, or bamboo fitted diapers that make your baby's bottom look totally cute; organic cotton, wool (naturally moisture resistant) diaper covers and fitted pants; and prefolds (flat diapers) that can be worn alone (some come with Velcro; some must be pinned) or tucked into diaper covers. Some covers and pants are made of, or coated with, moisture-resistant polyester or nylon, which is preferable to PVC!

www.amazon.com (for cloth diapers)

www.babyworks.com

www.betterforbabies.com

www.bumgenius.com

www.childorganics.com

www.clothdiaperoutlet.com (for Kissaluvs)

www.ebay.com (for cloth diapers)

www.ecodipes.com

www.vermontdiapercompany.com

For greener disposable diapers (non-chlorine-bleached, with some recycled content):

www.seventhgeneration.com (uses absorbent gel)

www.tushies.com (gel-free)

SAFER, GREENER TOYS

Babies take and treat their toys very personally and . . . well, intimately, chewing and mouthing them with abandon. Unfortunately, as most parents have become aware, there are some pretty toxic toys on the market. In 2008, more than 12.2 million products, including many Sesame Street/Fisher Price toys, even Elmo dolls, were recalled in the United States due to high levels of lead, which can cause learning problems.

Here's what you can do.

- Choose toys free of PVC, a plastic that commonly contains both phthalates and lead. Lego has been PVC-free for years. Other toy manufacturers that get on Greenpeace's PVC-free Toy Report Card are Brio, Gerber, International Play-things, Sassy, and Tiny Love.

- Choose toys made of wood certified as coming from well-managed forests by the Forest Stewardship Council (FSC), available at Toys "R" Us and from Hol-gate Toys.

- IKEA's nifty hardwood train sets for children age three and older use eco-friend-lier stainless steel and PVC-free plastic connectors.

- The Playstore has a wide range of certified organic cotton and natural wood toys for children of every age, including adorable, collectible animal figurines.

- See the PVC- and lead-free toy list at www.goodguide.com.

Before you shop, it's always a good idea to double-check the federal Consumer Product Safety Commission's recall list at www.cpsc.gov/cpscpub/prerel/cate gory/toy.html. Sometimes even green toys are recalled for safety violations, such as the three wooden items being voluntarily recalled from Earth Friendly Toys due to choking hazards: www.earthfriendlyllc.com/recall/.

SLEEP EASIER ON GREEN SHEETS

The following companies sell organic cotton (OC) sheets and pillowcases, many of which either are untreated or avoid the most harmful fabric finishes and dyes.

BED, BATH AND BEYOND: in addition to OC sheets, sells natural (untreated) and soy and bamboo bedding (www.bedbathandbeyond.com)

THE COMPANY STORE: sells an OC-covered down comforter, and bamboo blend sheets (www.thecompanystore.com)

COYUCHI: sells color-grown OC sheets (www.coyuchi.com)

GAIAM: offers OC and wool blankets, comforters, quilts, and mattress pads, and towels galore (www.gaiam.com)

NATIVE ORGANIC COTTON: sells OC bath and kitchen towels, and robes and aprons, too (www.nativeorganic.com)

POTTERY BARN: sells OC duvet covers, quilts, and coverlets (www.potterybarn.com)

WEST ELM: OC bath as well as bedding, throws, and more (www.westelm.com)

DIY: MATERIALS FOR SEWING AND KNITTING YOUR OWN ANYTHING

AHIMSA: Peace Silk; cruelty-free fabric produced without killing the moths (www.ahimsapeacesilk.com)

AURORA: silk, organic hemp, organic cotton, color-grown cotton, cruelty-free silk; also sells natural dye kits produced from plant, mineral, and insect sources available (www.aurorasilk.com)

CLOUD9: organic cotton fabric, chlorine-free and printed with certified OEKO-TEX dyes

EARTH FRIENDLY GOODS: hemp twill, muslin, cotton-blend, fleece, jersey, and knit fabric (www.earthfriendlygoods.com)

EARTHHUES: for dyes; SKAL-certified (www.earthues.com)

GREEN MOUNTAIN SPINNERY: certified organic wool yarn, produced with fleece from small regional sheep farms in Vermont (www.spinnery.com)

HEMP TRADERS: hemp fabric available by the yard or bolt (www.hemptraders.com)

LION: recycled cotton yarn, in seven sweet colors, including earth browns and birthday candle brights (www.lionbrand.com)

NEAR SEA NATURALS: organic cotton, organic wool, hemp and hemp blend woven and knit fabric; organic wool and organic cotton batting and stuffing, organic cotton elastic, thread, and trim also available. Plus, buttons made of nuts and recycled glass, as well as color-grown cotton and organic wool yarn (www.nearseanaturals.com)

TIERRA WOOLS: naturally dyed knitting yarns made from certified organically raised wool (www.handweavers.com)

WILD ROSE FARM: organic cotton fabrics and PCR fleece (www.wildrosefarm.coml; 1-218-562-4864)

For more information, log on to www.greenerpenny.com.

IV. *Transportation*

Not driving just one day a week can reduce your CO_2 emissions by about 8 pounds per week, or 400 pounds per year.

Walking, Biking, and Ride Sharing

13

ONE GREEN THING

Spend thirty minutes a day walking or cycling instead of driving.

Why? If every American did this, we'd cut CO_2 emissions by 64 million tons and lose 3 billion tons of excess body weight a year.

most-asked question

When traveling coast to coast, is it greener to fly or drive?

Flying, actually! Every individual passenger on an average, 2,500-mile cross-country plane trip is responsible for the emission of about 1,555 pounds of CO_2. That's heavy, yes, but driving that distance will just about double your emissions to 3,000 pounds! For more comparisons of the carbon emissions of different transport options, such as planes, trains, and motor vehicles, see the Union of Concerned Scientists' green travel report at www.ucsusa.org/assets/documents/clean_vehicles/greentravel_slick_opt_web.pdf.

another question

Is a hybrid such as the Prius, which can run on electric batteries as well as gas, the only car that's really green?

No. While it's true that the Toyota Prius, which gets an average 45 miles per gallon on the highway, is rated the most fuel-efficient car overall (see www.fueleconomy.gov), there are plenty of gasoline-only cars that get low mileage.

In any car, whether it's your old clunker or a Prius, you can vastly improve your mileage by taking simple steps such as keeping the engine tuned and the tires correctly inflated and driving at a steady speed.

GREENER TRAVEL

Take the train cross-country if you're not in a hurry (cost: 775 pounds of CO_2, half that of flying).

Take a plane cross-country if you're in a hurry (cost: 1,555 pounds of CO_2).

Compare prices online.

Carpool.

Take public transportation whenever possible.

If you're going to buy a car, used or new, aim for a minimum 30 miles per gallon, the federal standard for all new cars in 2011. See www.fueleconomy.gov.

Drive a car cross-country (cost: about 3,000 pounds of CO_2)

Drive from store to store and mall to mall to check prices.

Drive alone.

Always drive your own car; never catch a ride with others.

Drive a car that get under 20 miles per gallon.

Keep your engine tuned and your tires inflated and greatly improve your car's mileage.

Walking, Biking, and Ride Sharing

217

You're statistically less likely to die in a fatal plane crash than in a car crash.

The fewer cars on the road, the better our collective health. Vehicle combustion engines burn fossil fuels (gasoline or diesel) and emit smog, soot, and particulate matter containing toxic PAHs and carbon dioxide, all of which lead to respiratory disease.

better for the planet and the budget

Transportation produces 28 percent of U.S. greenhouse gas emissions. Each gallon of gasoline burned is responsible for the release of 28 pounds of CO_2, according to the Environmental Defense Fund (this includes the CO_2 released during the drilling and shipping of oil).

The average person drives almost 2,000 miles a year for shopping trips. If you cut down on driving by just 10 miles per week by combining errands, walking, or riding your bike, you could cut your CO_2 emissions by nearly 340 pounds per year.

CARS
Green Travel Tips

For more green driving tips, see
www.fueleconomy.gov/feg/maintain.shtml
and the Alliance to Save Energy's frequently updated
www.ase.org and www.ecodrivingusa.com.

- Carpool or telecommute to work. The average person drives about 3,000 miles to and from work every year. Not driving just one day a week can reduce your CO_2 emissions by about 8 pounds per week, or 400 pounds per year.

- Tune up and maintain your car. If you get your engine properly tuned and use the recommended grade of motor oil, you can cut CO_2 emissions and improve mileage by up to 6 percent (if you drive 12,000 miles per year at 20 miles per gallon—so you'll probably do even better).

- Check your tires. If all Americans drove with properly inflated tires, we'd cut gas consumption by 3.3 percent, saving up to about 13 million gallons of gas and reaping savings of $24 million a day (January 2009 average prices of $2 per gallon).

- Reduce driving speed and drive evenly.

- Reduce the things you carry: For every 100 pounds in or on your car, you lose 2 percent of your gas mileage.

Benefits to Driving More Slowly

Looking to buy a green car? Great references include the Green Car Journal, www.greencar.com and ACEEE's Green Guide to Cars and Trucks, www.aceee.org.

- CO_2 savings: about 1,500 pounds

- Cost-savings: about $288

- Fuel economy improves by almost 15 percent when you drive 65 miles per hour on the highway versus 75 mph. That translates to an average annual CO_2 savings of about 1,500 pounds, or about $288. Frequent acceleration and braking, rather than cruising at a steady speed, can lower your mileage by 33 percent. The bottom line: every 5 miles you drive above 60 mph costs you twenty cents more per gallon at the pump.

BEST SHOE LIST

Want to increase your walking and drive less? To get your walking regimen off to a good start, treat yourself to some shoes that tread more lightly on the Earth.

ADBUSTERS' BLACKSPOT SNEAKERS: 100 percent organic hemp uppers, made in a union shop (www.adbusters.org)

ADIDAS SLVR ECO-LABELED SHOES: made with hemp; company says it's working toward eliminating PVC (www.adidas.com)

ASICS RUNNING SHOES: look for the models labeled PVC-free (www.asics america.com)

BIRKENSTOCKS: cork soles are a renewable resource; they take back their footwear and resole it for you; last forever (www.birkenstockcentral.com)

BROOKS: uses FSC-certified paper for all packaging; Biomogo midsole supposedly biodegrades more quickly in landfills; 100 percent recycled laces, though not PCW; still, it's something (www.brooksrunning.com)

CHACO: PVC-free shoes, sandals, flip-flops (www.chacousa.com)

DAN.K. FOREST: organic hemp shoes (www.dankforest.com)

EARTH SHOES: 70 percent recycled material in their insoles (www.planet shoes.com)

END RUNNING SHOES: made with PCW recycled plastic, bamboo

HUNTER PVC-free, natural rubber "Wellies" (www.hunterboots.com)

KEDS GREEN LABEL SHOES: PVC-free sneakers made of 100 percent organic cotton, 20 percent recycled rubber outsoles, recycled insoles, recycled PET bottle laces (www.keds.com)

NIKE CONSIDERED: vegetable-based rather than toxic chrome leather tanning; fewer petroleum-based and more water-based, low-VOC solvents and adhesives; recycled laces; best of all, the company's take-back program recycles sneakers into athletic surfaces (www.nike.com and www.mikereusashoe.com)

PATAGONIA ECO SHOES: they are stitched, reducing the use of VOC-emitting glues and solvents that endanger worker health; in some shoes, you can replace the upper, frame, or outsole; leather is vegetable rather than chrome tanned, which is better for the environment and workers (www.patagonia.com)

RAWGANIQUE: hemp sandals for men and women (www.rawganique.com)

SIMPLE SHOES ECO SNEAKS and **GREEN TOE ECO** shoes: blend organic cotton and other natural fabrics, cork and PCW-recycled PET plastic (www.simpleshoes.com)

TIMBERLAND EARTHKEEPERS collection of shoes and boots: use natural rubber for soles, 30 percent of it recycled; and 70 percent recycled linings; company uses organic cotton in many of its fashions; most impressively, it has developed a Green Index that rates the carbon footprint of each of its shoes, which range from 22 to 220 pounds a pair. As one might guess, flip-flops have the lowest score and hiking boots the highest; leather, because of cows and methane, is the costliest material in terms of carbon (www.timberland.com)

TOMS: makes footwear for a greener tomorrow with hemp, recycled plastic bottles, and recycled rubber (www.tomsshoes.com)

For more information, log on to www.greenerpenny.com.

Walking, Biking, and Ride Sharing

WHERE TO DONATE OLD SHOES

The following organizations deliver wearable shoes to those who need them, including AIDS orphans in Africa.

www.hopeRuns.org

www.shoe4africa.org

www.shoebank.org

www.soles4souls.org

www.solesresponsibility.org

AIRPLANES

How to Fly Light (Including on Your Conscience)

TIP 1

Before you buy offsets for your travel, figure out your personal carbon footprint and that of your impending car or plane trip with the EPA's personal emissions calculator (www.epa.gov/climatechange/emissions/ind_calculator.htm/). You might very well be able to offset your trip yourself by reducing carbon emissions in other areas of your life.

A Carbon Weight-Loss Chart

Having lived most of my adult life on the East Coast, with friends and family in all parts of the globe, I can't escape air travel.

I figured there was plenty of carbon fat I could trim in my daily life to offset my next round-trip air flight. I confess: I'm really, really lazy when it comes to math, and totally unmotivated to do anything more than the most basic calculations. So, instead of calculating my exact carbon loads based on where my utility sourced its power, and totting up the exact wattage of the variety of lightbulbs I'd replaced, I picked some very basic steps and used generalized statistics that have been compiled for all Americans.

Here's what I'm doing, and what each step will, on average, save in pounds of carbon per year:

CHANGE MADE	POUNDS OF CARBON SAVED PER YEAR
Replace red meat with fish, eggs, and poultry.	950
Line-dry half my laundry loads.	723
Wash half the laundry in cold water.	72
Regularly clean the refrigerator coils, keep clutter off the top, and make sure that the door seal is snug.	700
Replace ten incandescent bulbs with CFLs.	550
Recycle all paper, plastic, and glass.	1,000
Increase the temperature on the air-conditioner in summer (it's a window unit with a thermostat, so I can't get the exact degrees, but if you can, set the thermostat at 78°F. when you're in, and turn off the AC when you go out).	up to 726
Lower the water heater thermostat to 120°F.	479
Plug the TV and cable box into a power strip and turn off when not in use (well, most of the time).	240
Cut four minutes off my shower time.	684
Walk instead of driving to work.	2, 750
TOTAL CARBON SAVED	as much as 8,717

I'm in the ballpark of almost offsetting the 9,000 pounds of carbon expended by three cross-country air trips!

If you must, or want to, purchase carbon offsets from companies that invest in renewable energy, such as wind and solar, tree planting, and other projects, to negate the carbon your actions emit. A single passenger traveling round trip from New York to Los Angeles will be responsible for emitting about 1,500 pounds of carbon, on average, according to the TerraPass carbon calculator at www.terrapass.com.

But before you buy, ask how much of your fee goes directly to fund projects, and how much to the company's own administrative costs.

Here are some of the more reputable offset companies:

Atmosfair (www.atmosfair.com)

Climate Friendly (www.climatefriendly.com)

Myclimate (www.myclimate.org)

TerraPass (www.terrapass.com)

Vermont-based NativeEnergy (www.nativeenergy.com)

If there's not a big price difference, fly airlines with good environmental records.

The nonprofit Climate Counts, which ranks companies by their efforts to combat climate change, recently began rating airlines and hotels. Northwest Airlines scored the highest—39 out of 100 points—followed by Southwest Airlines (37), American Airlines (35), and United Airlines (28). See www.climatecounts.org.

For comparative airfare price shopping, check out Fare Compare (www.farecompare.com).

Acknowledgments

I am forever indebted to:

Two visionaries—my green and gorgeous editor, Karyn Marcus, and Jeff Kleinman, the agent who never sleeps—without whose wit, vitality, and tireless work this book would never have happened, and the rest of the *Do One Green Thing* team: publishers Thomas Dunne, for giving us the green light, and Matthew Shear, for all the encouragement and help; John Murphy, Anne Marie Tallberg, Joe Goldschein, and Joan Higgins for their work in publicity and marketing the book; designer Rob Grom and illustrator Bill Garland for the delightful, personable cover; Michelle McMillian and Richard Oriolo for the page design that organized all this information so clearly and appealingly; Amelie Littell, David Stanford Burr, and Adriana Coada, production gurus; and Carolyn Vibbert, whose sparkling, distinctive illustrations set the perfect tone throughout.

Meryl Streep, for her wise counsel, generosity, and inspiration.

The loyal friends who've sustained me in countless ways: Franny and Philip White; Brook Hersey and Alex Delucca; Renee Khatami and Rick MacArthur; Donna Bulseco; Cynthia and John Russell; Jeanie Heifetz and Juris Jurjevics; Annic and Victor Navasky; Sarah Hill and Steve Cohen; Gail Harada; Alexis Gelber, Julio Vega, Dave and Sheila MacDonald, Sandi and Dell Hutchinson; Sheila Davies; Candy and Danny Murphy; Paul McRandle and Kirstin Chappell; Emily Main; Cara McCaffrey; Steve Hubbell and Tracy Tullis; Dee Jay and Donny Mailer; Patrique and Dominique Rennesson; Jean-Daniel and Catherine Matet; Jim Motavalli; Ellen Rosenbush, Lindsay Kurz; and the late Betsy Lydon.

The family who've supported my eco-ventures: Elizabeth Wallace; Bruce, Robert and Mark Pennybacker; Claire and David Wilson; John and Nick Kolivas; Ethan Won; Alex Wallace; Nancy Lungren; Ray Watts; and the late Lawrence and Mary Kang, Miles Pennybacker, Donald Wallace, Jr., and Anne "Penny" Watts.

My collective conscience—the editorial advisors who have always given the time and effort to make sure I get it right: Luz Claudio, Ph.D.; David Steinman; Joan Gussow, Ph.D.; Fred Kirschenman, Ph.D.; Harvey Karp, M.D.; Philip Landrigan, M.D.; Herb Needleman, M.D.; Rachel Newman; Ricky Perera, Ph.D.; Maria Rodale; and Bob Scowcroft.

All the very smart readers whose questions and ideas make this work an endless pleasure.

Thank you, one and all!

Resources

Contact any of the following leading environmental and health nonprofit and governmental organizations for further information and to find out how to get involved.

If you want more detailed and updated information on the topics discussed in this book, visit these linked websites: OneGreenThingtheBook.com and GreenerPenny.com, where you can read articles and blogs, ask me questions, sign up for free weekly e-newsletters, and find downloadable shopping lists, cell phone shopping applications, and more.

The resources listed here, arranged by topic, include the leading environmental science, health, conservation, eco-label verification, and consumer protection organizations whose research and dedication inform this book. Also included are government agencies and a list of books, magazines, and websites I regularly tap into, and highly recommend.

Groups active in many environmental issues across the board are listed as "Multitaskers."

Drinking Water

Bottled Water
Earth Policy Institute (www.earth-policy.org)
Food and Water Watch (www.foodandwaterwatch.org/water)
Pacific Institute (www.pacinst.org)

Tap Water
National tap water databases (listing contaminants by region): Environmental Protection Agency
   (www.epa.gov/safewater/dwinfo/index.html) and Environmental Working Group
   (www.ewg.org/tapwater/yourwater/)
List of third-party-certified water filters (www.nsf.org/certified/consumer/listings_results.asp)
Tips for choosing water filters (www.nrdc.org/water/drinking/gfilters.asp
   scribd.com/doc/5107459/Water-Filtration-Guide)
Watershed and waterways protection: (www.epa.gov/adopt/); Waterkeeper Alliance (www.water
   keeper.org); Riverkeeper (www.riverkeeper.org)

Food and Agriculture

Food and Drink Labels to Look For
 American Grassfed Association
(www.americangrassfed.org)

 Animal Welfare Approved
(www.animalwelfareapproved.org)

Bird Friendly, Smithsonian Migratory Bird Center (coffee)
(www.nationalzoo.si.edu)

Demeter Biodynamic
(www.demeter-usa.org)

 Fair Trade Certified (Transfair USA)
(www.transfairusa.org)

 Fair Trade Federation
(www.fairtradefederation.org)

 The Food Alliance
(www.foodalliance.org)

 Humane Farm Animal Care (www.certifiedhumane.org)

 LIVE certified sustainable (wine)
(www.liveinc.org/)

 Protected Harvest
(www.protectedharvest.org)

 The Rainforest Alliance
(www.ra.org)

 Salmon Safe
(www.salmonsafe.or)

USDA Organic
(www.ams.usda.gov/NOP)

Research and Publications on Organic and Other Standards in Sustainable Agriculture
Association of Family Farms (www.familyfood.net)
Institute for Agriculture and Trade Policy (www.iatp.org)
Integrated Pest Management Institute (www.ipminstitute.org)
Leopold Institute for Sustainable Agriculture (www.leopold.iastate.edu)
Organic Consumers Association (www.organicconsumers.org)
Organic Trade Association (www.ota.org)

Finding Sustainably Grown Food
Eat Well Guide (www.eatwellguide.org)
Eat Wild (pasture-raised animal products) (www.eatwild.com)
Local Harvest (www.localharvest.org)
Sustainable Table (www.sustainabletable.org)
U.S. Department of Agriculture farmers' market locator (www.apps.ams.usda.gov/FarmersMarkets/)

Chefs Collaborative (www.chefscollaborative.org)

Chez Panisse Foundation's Edible Schoolyard (www.edibleschoolyard.org)

Preserving Heirloom, Traditional and Artisanal Plant and Animal Foods
Slow Food USA (www.slowfoodusa.org)

Genetically Engineered/Modified Foods and Global Warming and Agriculture
Union of Concerned Scientists (www.ucsusa.org)
Worldwatch Institute (www.worldwatch.org)

Food Containers and Cookware

Plastic Containers

 Biodegradable Products Institute/USA Composting Council "Compostable" label (www.bpiworld.org)

Teflon cookware chemicals (www.ewg.org)
Washington Toxics Coalition
   (www.watoxics.org/safer-products/choosing-safer-products-lunchboxes-and-food-storage)

Pesticides and Alternatives

Beyond Pesticides (www.beyondpesticides.org)
Bio-Integral Research Center (www.birc.org)
Extension Toxicology Network: university USDA extensions pesticides database
   (www.extoxnet.orst.edu/)
Local USDA cooperative extensions (www.csrees.usda.gov/extension)
Northeast Organic Farming Association (www.organiclandcare.net)
Northwest Coalition for Alternatives to Pesticides (www.pesticide.org)
Pesticide Action Network North America (www.panna.org) and pesticides database
   (www.pesticideinfo.org)
Washington Toxics Coalition (www.watoxics.org)

Seafood

Sustainable, Safer Choices
Blue Ocean Institute Guide to Ocean-Friendly Seafood (www.blueocean.org and www.fishphone.org)
Environmental Defense Fund Seafood Selector (www.edf.org)
The Fish List (www.thefishlist.org) Food and Water Watch seafood guide (www.foodandwaterwatch.org)
Monterey Bay Aquarium Seafood Watch seafood guides (www.mbayaq.org)

Sustainable Seafood Labels

Eco Fish
(www.ecofish.com)

Fish farming (www.foodandwaterwatch.org/fish/fish-farming)

 Marine Stewardship Council
(www.msc.org)

Pew Oceans Commission reports (www.pewtrusts.org)

Mercury and Other Pollutants in Seafood

Environmental Defense Fund health alert list (mercury and PCBs)
(www.edf.org/page.cfm?tagID=17694)

Environmental Protection Agency mercury advisory (www.epa.gov/waterscience/fish/advice/fact
sheet.html)

Environmental Working Group mercury in tuna calculator (www.ewg.org)

Local fish advisories by state and water body (www.epa.gov/waterscience/fish/)

U.S. Food and Drug Administration mercury levels in fish and shellfish chart
(www.cfsan.fda.gov/~frf/sea-mehg.html cfsan.fda.gov)

Ocean/Beach Environment Protection

Oceana (www.oceana.org)

Surfrider Foundation (www.surfrider.org)

Electricity, Energy, and Greenhouse Gases

American Council for an Energy Efficient Economy (www.aceee.org)

Consortium for Energy Efficiency (www.ceel.org)

Database of state incentives for renewable energy (www.dsireusa.org)

 Energy Guide label
(www.1.eere.energy.gov/consumer/tips/energyguide.html)

 Energy Star label
(www.energystar.gov)

Environmental Defense's Lightbulb Selector (www.edf.org)

Green Power Options: choosing alternative energy providers
(www.eere.energy.gov/greenpower/buying)

Rocky Mountain Institute (www.rmi.org)

U.S. Department of Energy Office of Energy Efficiency and Renewable Energy
(www.eere.energy.gov/consumer)

Global Warming/Climate Change

Consumers Union Greener Choices global warming and your home
(www.greenerchoices.org)

Earth Institute at Columbia University (www.climate.columbia.edu/)

Environmental Defense Fund tips for a low carbon lifestyle (www.edf.org)

Intergovernmental Panel on Climate Change (www.ipcc.ch/)

Stanford University Woods Institute for the Environment (www.woods.stanford.edu350.org)

Stop Global Warming (www.stopglobalwarming.org)

Union of Concerned Scientists (www.ucsusa.org)

Electronics Manufacturing/Disposal

Basel Action Network (www.ban.org)

Electronic Product Environmental Assessment Tool, EPEAT (www.epeat.net)

Greenpeace Guide to Greener Electronics (www.greenpeace.org/usa)

Silicon Valley Toxics Coalition (www.etoxics.org)

Water Saving

Alliance for Water Efficiency (www.allianceforwaterefficiency.org)

H2OUSE Water Saver Home (www.h2ouse.net)

 Water Sense label and standards
(www.epa.gov/watersense)

Breathing Cleaner Air

Air quality index (www.airnow.gov)

American Lung Association (www.lungusa.org)

California Air Resources Board (www.arb.ca.gov)

Environmental Health

Breast Cancer Fund (www.breastcancerfund.org)

Center for Children's Health and the Environment, Mount Sinai School of Medicine
(www.childenvironment.org)

Centers for Disease Control and Prevention (www.cdc.gov)

Columbia Center for Children's Environmental Health, Columbia University
(www.mailman.columbia.edu/ccceh/index.html)

Environmental Health News (www.environmentalhealthnews.org)

Environmental Health Perspectives (www.ehponline.org)

Harvard Center for Health and the Global Environment (www.chge.med.harvard.edu)

Health Care Without Harm (www.noharm.org)

Healthy Child, Healthy World (www.healthychild.org)

National Institute of Environmental Health Sciences (www.niehs.nih.gov)

Silent Spring Institute (www.silentspring.org)

Household Cleaning, and Avoiding VOCs

Building Green, Inc. (www.buildinggreen.com)

Center for Health, Environment, and Justice vinyl shower curtain VOCs report (www.chej.org/show
  ercurtainreport/)

Consumers Union Eco-labels project (www.greenerchoices.org/eco-labels)

 EcoLogo seal
(www.ecologo.org)

 EPA Design for Environment Seal

 Green Seal

National Library of Medicine Household Products Database (www.householdproducts.nlm.nih.gov)

Scientific Certification Systems, certifying VOC-free pressed woods (www.scsccrtified.com)

U.S. Green Building Council (www.usgbc.org)

Women's Voices for the Earth (www.womenandenvironment.org/greenclean)

Personal Care

 BDIH seal

Campaign for Safe Cosmetics (www.safecosmetics.org)

 Certified Vegan

 Ecocert

 Leaping Bunny

Not Too Pretty/Skin Deep Cosmetics Safety Database, searchable by brands, products,
  and ingredients (www.cosmeticsdatabase.org)

 NPA

Oasis

Organic Consumers Association (www.organicconsumers.org/bodycare/index.cfm)

 Soil Association

Recycling, Composting, and Waste

Craigslist (www.craigslist.org)
Earth911 (www.earth911.com)

 Forrest Stewardship Council

Freecycle (www.freecycle.org)
Kokua Hawaii Foundation (www.kokuahawaiifoundation.org)
National Recycling Coalition (www.nrc-recycle.org)
Organic Gardening magazine (www.organicgardening.com)
Public Interest Research Groups (www.uspirg.org/)
Rechargeable Battery Recycling Corporation (www.rbrc.org)

 Scientific Certification Systems

Terracycle (www.terracycle.net)
U.S. Composting Council (www.compostingcouncil.org)

Product Life Cycles

 Cradle to Cradle label (www.c2ccertified.com)
from McDonough Braungart (www.mbdc.com)

Patagonia's Footprint Chronicles, tracking environmental and social impact of its products
(www.patagonia.com/web/us/footprint/index.jsp)
University of Michigan Center for Sustainable Systems: works with companies in calculating
carbon footprint of products (www.css.snre.umich.edu/)

Apparel

Earth Pledge Future Fashion project, green fashion shows (www.earthpledge.org/ff)

 Fair Trade Certified
(www.transfairusa.org)

 Fair Trade Federation
(www.fairtradefederation.org)

Fair Trade Mark: seal administered by the Fair Trade Foundation, which monitors workplaces using
independent third parties (www.fairtrade.net/the_fairtrade_mark.html)

Green America Approved: companies displaying this seal have met the socially responsible, fair trade or green standards set by Green America, formerly Co-Op America (www.coopamerica.org/greenbusiness/sealofapproval.cfm)

National Association of Diaper Services (www.diapernet.org)
Organic Consumers Association (www.organicconsumers.org/clothes/index.cfm)
Organic Trade Association organic wool information (www.ota.com/OrganicWool.html)
Sustainable Cotton Project (www.sustainablecotton.org/)

 U.S. Consumer Products Safety Commission fire retardancy seal (www.cpsc.gov)

Wildlife/Ecosystem/Open Space Protection

Convention on International Trade in Endangered Species (www.cites.org)
National Audubon Society (www.audubon.org)
National Wildlife Federation (www.nwf.org)
The Nature Conservancy (www.tnc.org)
Trust for Public Land (www.tpl.org)
World Wildlife Fund (www.wwf.org)

Transportation

ACEEE Green Guide to Cars and Trucks (www.aceee.org)
Alliance to Save Energy (www.ase.org)
Fuel Economy (www.fueleconomy.gov)
Green Car Journal (www.greencar.com)
Union of Concerned Scientists (www.ucsusa.org)

Ecotourism

Conservation International (www.conservation.org)
International Ecotourism Society (www.ecotourism.org)
Rainforest Alliance (www.ra.org)

Multitaskers

The following leading groups have programs dealing with a variety of the issues mentioned in this resource list:

Earth Justice (www.earthjustice.com)
Earth Pledge (www.earthpledge.org)
Environmental Defense Fund (www.edf.org)
Environmental Working Group (www.ewg.org)
Friends of the Earth (www.foe.org)

Greenpeace (www.greenpeaceusa.org)
Natural Resources Defense Council (www.nrdc.org)
Sierra Club (www.sierraclub.org)
Worldwatch Institute (www.worldwatch.org)
United Nations Environment Programme (www.unep.org)

Groups Vetting Green/Organic Products and Claims

Consumers Union, publisher of *Consumer Reports* and *Shop Smart* (www.consumersunion.org)
Consumers Union Greener Choices (www.greenerchoices.org and www.eco-labels.org)
Green America (formerly Co-Op America) (www.coopamerica.org)
Organic Consumers Association (www.organicconsumers.org)

Recommended Reading

Websites and Magazines

Body + Soul: Wellness equals green living in this beautiful magazine (www.bodyandsoulmag.com).

The Daily Green: Some of my favorite eco-bloggers post to this hip, newsy site, which is particularly strong on food and home renovation tips (www.thedailygreen.com).

Good magazine: Covering environmental technology and news, with a bow to culture and community, this well-rounded print and online source is provocative and timely (www.good.is/).

E: The Environmental Magazine: The gray-green lady of eco-news, E has kept readers entertained and engaged since 1989 (www.emagazine.com).

Elle: Regularly covers green cosmetic, fashion, and lifestyle trends—with flair (www.elle.com).

Grist: Eco-advocacy with an attitude, this site includes terrific news, blogs, and, of course, Umbra, whom you can ask anything (www.grist.org).

Harper's: Very strong, in-depth and unconventional environmental and social justice investigative reporting (www.harpers.org).

Huffington Post (www.huffingtonpost.com/green)

Mothering magazine: Thoughtful and practical advice for those raising the next generation, including updates on the diaper debate, nursing support groups, and healthy baby diets (www.mothering mag.com).

Mother Jones: Great investigative reporting, including mercury poisoning case studies and the plight of the seas (www.motherjones.com).

Natural Home: The gorgeous shelter book for green-minded nesters, this one includes plenty of budget and decorating tips (www.naturalhomemagazine.com).

Ode: Cheery and witty, this magazine is positive that we can and will do the right thing (www.odemagazine.com).

OnEarth magazine: Featuring poetry and investigative science reporting on global issues, from the tar sands of Canada to the melting Arctic to hormone-disrupting chemicals, this magazine is yet another reason to join the NRDC, its home (www.www.onearth.org).

Orion magazine: Featuring poetry, philosophy, photographs, this is a mindful and inspiring magazine (www.orion.org).

Real Simple: Green's now a regular feature here, with an A-to-Z recycling guide, green cleaning tips, and more (www.realsimple.com).

Sierra magazine: This green glossy profiles people working for change in their communities and pays close attention to social welfare and the environmental conservation for which its publisher, The Sierra Club, is justly famous. Plus, it covers consumer products and food, and it's where you can chat with Mr. Green (www.sierraclub.org).

The Nation: Its environmental, fair labor, and health reporting can't be beat (www.thenation.com).

The New Yorker: Published two great global warming exposes, Elizabeth Kolbert's *Field Notes from a Catastrophe* and Bill McKibben's *The End of Nature* in their entirety; need we say more? (www.the newyorker.com).

Treehugger: These killer blogs are the place to look for the latest green products and inventions (www.treehugger.com).

Vegetarian Times: Takes an in-depth look at sustaining yourself on a sustainable diet (www.vegetari antimes.com).

Yoga Journal: You don't even have to do the poses; just looking at this serene magazine makes you feel good (www.yogajournal.com).

Books

Brower, Michael, and Warren Leon. *The Consumer's Guide to Effective Environmental Choices: Practical Advice from the Union of Concerned Scientists*. Three Rivers Press, 1999.

David, Laurie. *Stop Global Warming: The Solution Is You!* Fulcrum, 2006.

Dolan, Deirdre, and Alexandra Zissu. *The Complete Organic Pregnancy*. HarperCollins, 2006.

Gavigan, Christopher. *Healthy Child, Healthy World*. Plume, 2009.

Gore, Al. *An Inconvenient Truth*. Viking, 2006.

Gussow, Joan. *This Organic Life: Confessions of a Suburban Homesteader*. Chelsea Green, 2001.

Helvarg, David. *Blue Frontier: Dispatches from America's Ocean Wilderness*. Sierra Club Books, 2006.

Horn, Miriam, and Fred Krupp. *Earth: the Sequel: The Race to Reinvent Energy and Stop Global Warming*. Norton, 2008.

Kingsolver, Barbara, Camille Kingsolver, and Steven L. Hopp. *Animal, Vegetable, Mineral*. Harper-Collins, 2007.

Kolbert, Elizabeth, *Field Notes from a Catastrophe*, Bloomsbury USA, 2008.

Imus, Deirdre, *The Essential Green You!* Simon & Schuster, 2008.

———*Growing Up Green!* Simon & Schuster, 2008.

———*Green This! Greening Your Cleaning*, Simon & Schuster, 2007.

Landrigan, Philip J., M.D., Herbert L. Needleman, M.D., and Mary M. Landrigan, M.P.A. *Raising Healthy Children in a Toxic World*, Rodale, 2002.

McDonough, William, and Michael Braungart. *Cradle to Cradle: Rethinking the Way We Make Things*. North Point Press, 2002.

McKibben, Bill. *The End of Nature*. Knopf, 1989.

———. *Deep Economy*, Times Books, 2007.

Malkan, Stacy. *Not Just a Pretty Face: The Ugly Side of the Beauty Industry*. New Society Publishers, 2007.

Motavalli, Jim, Brian Howard, and Doug Moss. *Green Living: The E. Magazine Handbook for Living Lightly on the Earth*. Plume, 2005.

Nestle, Marion. *What to Eat*. North Point Press, 2007.

Newman, Nell, and Joseph D'Agnese. *The Newman's Own Organics Guide to the Good Life*. Villard, 2003.

Pennybacker, Mindy, and Aisha Ikramuddin. *Mothers and Others for a Livable Planet Guide to Natural Baby Care*. John Wiley and Sons, 1999.

Petrini, Carlo. *Slow Food*. Columbia University Press, 2003.

Pollan, Michael. *The Omnivore's Dilemma*, 2006.

———. *In Defense of Food*. Penguin, 2008.

Revkin, Andrew C. *The North Pole Was Here*. Kingfisher, 2007.

Rogers, Elizabeth, and Thomas Kostigen. *The Green Book*. Three Rivers Press, 2008.

Royte, Elizabeth. *Garbage Land*. Little, Brown & Co., 2005.

———. *Bottlemania*. Bloomsbury USA, 2008.

Schapiro, Mark. *Exposed: The Toxic Chemistry of Everyday Products and What's at Stake for American Power*. Chelsea Green, 2007.

Schildgen, Bob. *Hey, Mr. Green*. Sierra Club Books, 2008.

Schlosser, Eric. *Fast Food Nation*. Houghton Mifflin, 2001.

Steinman, David. *Safe Trip to Eden: 10 Steps to Save Planet Earth*. Thunder's Mouth, 2007.

You can help protect the planet and your health by taking any (or all) of the following steps:

- Get involved in protecting your watershed and the purity of your tap water, which flows from it. To learn about water sources in your region, go to www.epa.gov/owow/watershed/region/.

- Find out your ecological footprint by taking the appealing, thought-provoking educational quiz at the site Ecological Footprint (www.myfootprint.org), which isn't limited to determining your carbon footprint, but also measures your impact in terms of the food and goods and services you consume, and your housing. It even asks about cleaning products and where you shop. Finally, it tells you how much acreage would be required to support your footprint. Although I scored lower than the national average in every category except my food footprint, if everyone on Earth lived my lifestyle, we'd need 4.2 Earths to support us! Luckily, the quiz also lets you read on in each category for ideas on how to reduce your footprint. It's quiet, sane, and oddly comforting.

- For anti-water privatization initiatives, see www.thinkoutsidethebottle.org.

- The Environmental Working Group is demanding that the EPA reduce its Energy Star requirement of no more than 5 milligrams of mercury per CFL, and that manufacturers list mercury content on labels. EWG notes that many manufacturers now voluntarily attain a mercury content as low as 1 milligram. You can help by sending a letter to the EPA from the "Lightbulb Campaign" page at www.ewg.org.

- Join the international campaign to reduce greenhouse gases to 350 parts per million, the level at which the climate can be stabilized. Go to www.350.org, an outgrowth of Bill McKibben's successful 2007 "Step It Up" college campus initiative, and www.stopglobalwarming.org.

- Get off catalog lists, and keep off new mailing lists, by subscribing to www.greendimes.com for $3 per month. They also plant a tree in your name in deforested areas.

- Stop direct mail being sent to you for only $1 at www.dmaconsumers.org/cgi/offmailing.

- No curbside recycling? If your town does not pick up plastics, paper, metal or glass for recycling put out by the curb, contact your state Public Interest Research Group (PIRG), which you can find at www.uspirg.org/about-us/the-state-pirgs, to help you and your neighbors get a program going.

Glossary

1,4 dioxane: a contaminant classified as a known carcinogen by the California Environmental Protection Agency; by-product that can be created by a chemical process known as ethoxylation, which takes place during formulation of some cleaning and personal care products.

Alkyphenol ethoxylates (APEs): synthetic sudsing chemicals, or surfactants, used in detergents, that have been implicated in hormone disruption in fish and amphibians in APE-contaminated waters.

Carbon footprint: A measure of each person's contribution to global warming. It's the amount of greenhouse gases (GHG), measured in tons, that an individual is responsible for releasing every year. In our burning of fossil fuels (carbon) for transportation and powering our homes, the average American "generates" at least 20 tons of CO_2 every year—about the same amount as three new cars emit a year, according to the Union of Concerned Scientists. Adding in the GHG released in the production and shipping of the food and other products we consume gives a fuller—and weightier—picture of our overall footprint. While it's named after carbon dioxide (CO_2), the main greenhouse gas, a carbon footprint also takes into account equivalent warming caused by other GHGs, principally nitrous oxide and methane.

Carbon offsets: a financial instrument meant to counterbalance the release of carbon dioxide and other GHGs. Everyone, from companies to individuals, can neutralize the carbon they emit by purchasing offsets from companies who implement projects such as planting trees or developing renewable energy sources that reduce emissions.

Compact fluorescent light (CFL): a light that is 75 percent more efficient and will burn ten times longer than an incandescent lightbulb.

Cradle2Cradle: a term coined by top green architect William McDonough and his chemist business partner, Michael Braumgart, for "closed-loop" products. They now have begun certifying a variety of products that meet their standards for complete biodegradability. See www.mbdc.com.

Ethoxylated chemicals: these include alkyphenol ethoxylates (APEs) and sodium laureth sulfate (SLES); can contaminate products with 1,4 dioxane, a cancer-causing chemical.

Food Miles: The distance food travels from where it was grown to your plate.

Foodshed: along the same lines as a watershed, it's the area where local farms produce the food that comes to your farmers' market.

Genetic engineering/genetic modification: also known as transgenics, or gene splicing, this biotechnology technique permits genes for different traits, such as herbicide resistance, to be moved between unrelated organisms that could not otherwise interbreed. The resulting seeds or plants are known as genetically engineered or genetically modified organisms (GMOs). GE/GM is barred from organic agriculture because GMOs are "made with techniques that alter the molecular or cell biology of an organism by means that are not possible under natural conditions," according to the National Organic Standards Board, which advises the USDA in determining the criteria for organic qualification.

Glycol ethers: synthetic degreasers that emit powerful fumes that can cause respiratory distress, dizziness, and, with high exposures over the long term, nervous system harm.

Greenhouse gases (GHG): any of the various gaseous compounds that absorb radiation, trap heat in the atmosphere, and contribute to global warming. There are three principal GHGs:

- Carbon dioxide (CO_2): a heavy, colorless gas released by burning fossil fuels—petroleum, coal, and gas—in our vehicles and by power plants that supply electricity to our businesses, schools, and homes.

- Methane (CH_4): a gas 23 times as potent as CO_2, methane is released by cattle, sheep, and goats when they belch and so forth, it's also emitted by decomposing organic matter in land-fills.

- Nitrous Oxide (N_2O): This gas, which is 296 times more potent than CO_2, is released by syn-thetic nitrogen fertilizers made from natural gas, as well as through combustion of fossil fuels by industry and in vehicle engines.

Hormone (or endocrine) disrupters: predominantly man-made, but sometimes natural, substances that imitate the action of the hormone estrogen in the body. Some effects can include stimulating the growth of breast cancer cells and feminizing reproductive organs in males.

Kilowatt hour (kWh): the measurement of 1,000 watts of energy used in an hour; the measurement the utility company uses to charge us.

Light-emitting diodes (LEDs): tiny points of light first used in flashlights and strings for Christmas trees and out of doors; LEDs are now being clustered into lightbulbs for indoor lamp designs.

Locavore: a person who prefers local food; the Oxford English Dictionary word of the year in 2007.

Nony phenol (NPE): a type of alkyphenol ethoxylate (APE) suspected of interfering with normal hormonal systems and development; currently of most concern in cleaning, laundry, and some soap and shampoo products.

Phosphates: chemicals in detergents that harm ecosystems downstream by stimulating the growth of algae, which rob water bodies of oxygen, killing fish.

Product lifecycle: Whether it's clothing or computers, a product's lifecycle is its environmental impact at every stage, from cradle to grave. The greenest product has a lifecycle that's cradle to cradle, coming to a fully reusable, biodegradable end, or closed loop.

Sustainable: a process that can be repeated over and over without negative environmental effects or impossibly high costs to anyone involved.

Volatile organic compounds (VOCs): strong, irritating, and sometimes toxic fumes that readily evap-orate, or "offgas," from mostly petroleum-derived chemicals in cleaning solvents, glues, finishes, paints, and pesticides. Some strong plant-based solvents, typically citrus or pine, also emit VOCs.

Notes

Overview

xviii Eco anxiety: A term for feelings of angst, guilt, and being overwhelmed by environmental problems, from "Eco Anxiety," R. O. Blechman, *New York Times Magazine,* April 20, 2008.

xv Growth in farmers' markets: 6.8 percent increase from 2006 to 2008, at www.ams.USDA.gov/amsv1.0/getfile?dDocName=STELPRDC5072472&acct=frmrdirmkt.

xv Double-digit growth in U.S. marketplaces for: organic food (17 percent in 2008, average 22–23 percent annually from 1995 to 2007), Organic Trade Association, at www.ota.org; fair-trade-certified food (10 percent growth in 2008), at www.transfairusa.org; and global growth in food and nonfood fair trade marketplace (47 percent growth from 2006 to 2007), at www.ftsla.org/publicationsPress/expowest09_presentations/expowest_ecolabels_barill.pdf.

xv Growth in natural personal care products (13 percent growth in 2008): "Growth for the Natural Product Segment Outpaces General Personal Care Market by a Landslide," Kline Group Report, 2008, at www.klinegroup.com/news/natural_organic_care_grayson.asp.

1. Drinking Water

3–4 Bottled water's footprint in fossil fuels, water, energy, greenhouse gases: The Pacific Institute and Earth Policy Institute's 2007 reports on bottled water's environmental and energy impacts, at www.pacinst.org/topics/water_and_sustainability/bottled_water/bottled_water_and_energy.html; earth-policy.org/Updates/2007/Update68.htm.

4–5 Bottled water is less strictly regulated than municipal tap water: Food and Water Watch, "Bottled Water: Illusions of Purity," 2007 report, at www.foodandwaterwatch.org/water/bottled/ bottled-water-illusions-of-purity; and the Environmental Working Group, www.ewg.org/newsrelease/FDA-Should-Adopt-EPA-Tap-Water-Health-Goals-for-Bottled-Water.

5 Tests have found many unhealthy contaminants in bottled water: In 2008, EWG found 39 contaminants in samples of 10 brands of bottled water, at www.ewg.org/reports/bottledwater. In 1999, the Natural Resources Defense Council studied 1,000 samples from 103 brands of bottled water, and found that samples from one third of the brands had levels of contaminants that exceeded state or industry standards. The NRDC also found that tap water is more strictly regulated than bottled, noting that most cities regularly test municipal water supplies for contamination by E. coli, cryptosporidium, and giardia, and for toxic chemicals, at www.nrdc.org/water/drinking/bw/nbw.asp. Further, water utilities are required by law to send water quality reports to all consumers, notifying us of any contaminant levels in excess of EPA safety standards; there is no such reporting requirement for bottled water.

5–6 For tap water contaminants: NRDC's 2003 report on public drinking water in nineteen large U.S. cities, which concluded that only one, Chicago, had "excellent" water quality. Five cities were rated "good"; eight, "fair"; and five, "poor"; EWG's 2005 report, www.ewg.org/tapwater/findings.php.

5 Waste caused by water bottles: Container Recycling Institute, 2006, at www.container-recy cling. org/plasfact/bottledwater.htm.

6 Carbon filters remove most common contaminants: www.nrdc.org/water/drinking/gfilters.asp.

5 Worldwide, 1.1 billion people lack safe drinking water: United Nations Task Force on Water and Sanitation's 2006 report, www.unwater.org/wwdr?-news2.html.

5–6 Privatization threat: Maud Barlow, UN senior adviser on water issues, in interview with *Wall Street Journal*, Nov. 8, 2008, and at www.wsj.com/article/SB122610638674310287.html.

5 Limited supply of accessible fresh water: University of Michigan, www.globalchange.umich. edu/globalchange2/current/lectures/freshwater_supply/freshwater.html.

8–9 Developmental risks posed to human infants by Bisphenol-A: National Toxicology Program final report on BPA, www.niehs.nih.gov/news/releases/2008/bisphenol-a.cfm.

9 Pregnant women should avoid exposure: Quote from Dr. Len Ritter, professor at University of Guelph and lead researcher in 2008 study showing BPA to be at higher concentrations in bodies of newborns than of adults, in *The Star*, www.thestar.com/News/Canada/article/591028BPA.

9 BPA linked to cardiovascular disease and diabetes in adults: *Journal of the American Medical Association* 300, no. 11 (Sept. 2008): 1303–10; online at www.jama.ama-assn.org/cgi/content /full/300/ 11/1303.

10 Phthalates and other hormone-imitating chemicals may be leaking from PET and other plastic bottles over time: "Bottled Water May Contain 'Hormones': Plastics," by Janet Raloff, *Science News*, March 7, 2009, online at www.sciencenews.org/view/generic/id/41628/title /Science_% 2B_the_Public_ Bottled_water_may_contain_%E2%80%98hormones%E2%80%99_Plastics; see also www.nrdc.org/water/drinking/qbw.asp.

8 BPA can leach from polycarbonate (PC) baby bottles: www.environmentcalifornia.org/reports/ environmental-health/environmental-health-reports/toxic-baby-bottles.

8, 12 BPA can leach from PC water bottles: "Bye-Bye, BPA," on GreenerPenny blog, at www.green erpenny.blogspot.com/2007/08/bye-bye-bpa.html; David Biello, "Plastic Not Fantastic," *Scientific American*, at www.scientificamerican.com/article.cfm?id=plastic-not-fantastic-with-bisphenol-a.

10–11 Information on resins used, and the recyclability of plastics by code number: American Chemistry Council, www.americanchemistry.com.

10–11 Bioplastics: "Plastics Graduate to Green," Paul McRandle, The Green Guide, www.e-green guide.net/doc/114/pla.

10 Toxicity of polyvinyl chloride plastic (PVC): Tufts University Global Development and Environment Institute, "The Economics of Phasing Out PVC," by Frank Ackerman and Rachel Massey, pp. 1, 4, 11; online at www.healthybuilding.net/pvc/Economics_Of_Phasing_ Out_PVC.pdf .

10–11 Toxicity of PVC, polystyrene (PS), and other plastics: Greenpeace report, www.archive.green-peace.org/toxics/pvcdatabase/bad.html; see also information on polystyrene Styrofoam at www.styrophobia.com.

2. Produce

16 Children's proportionately greater exposure to pesticides, and the risks thereof, compared with adults: "Pesticides in the Diets of Infants and Children," National Academies Press, 1993, www.books.nap.edu/openbook.php?record_id=2126.

18 Every day, more than 600,000 children ages 1 to 5 eat an unsafe dose of neurotoxic organophosphate insecticides: EWG report, Wiles et al., "How 'Bout Them Apples? Pesticides in Children's Food," 1999, www.ewg.org/files/apples.pdf.

18 Pesticide residues in produce most frequently eaten by children: Consumers Union, Groth et al., "Pesticide Residues Still Too High in Children's Foods," 2000, www.consumersunion.org /pub/ core_food_safety/002324.html; UN Food and Agriculture Organization report, www.fao.org/DO CREP/005/Y4137E/y4137e01.htm.

19 Organic agriculture standards: USDA National Organic Program, list of allowed and prohibited substances, www.ams.usda.gov/AMSv1.0/ams.fetchTemplateData.do?template=Tem plateA&nav ID=NationalOrganicProgram&leftNav=NationalOrganicProgram&page=NOPNationalOrganic ProgramHome&acct=nop.

18–19 Overview of toxic pesticides used on U.S. and international food crops: Organic Trade Association, www.ota.com/organic/benefits/health.html; National Environmental Education Foundation, www.neefusa.org/pdf/pest/A%20Pesticide%20Primer,%20pp%2011-17% 20Education.pdf.

18 940 million pounds of chemical pesticides were applied to U.S. crops in 2000, of which 40 percent were chemicals (organophosphates, carbamates, probable or possible carcinogens) linked to cancer or nervous system harm: Organic Trade Association, www.theorganic pages.com/topo/organic /benefits/health.html?fromOta=1&OtaImage=1.

18 Two-thirds fewer pesticides on organic than conventionally grown produce: Consumers Union study, Groth et al., "Pesticide Residues Still Too High in Children's Foods," 2000, www.consumer sunion.org/pub/core_food_safety/002324.html.

18 Reducing exposure to pesticides through organic: A recent study found that eating fresh produce is the major source of exposure to organophosphate pesticides in young children's bodies; but the good news is that when the children's diets were switched to organic produce for five days, levels of pesticide residue in their urine fell to virtually undetectable levels. Lu et al., "Dietary Intake and Its Contribution to Longitudinal Organophosphate Pesticide Exposure in Urban/Suburban Children," *Environmental Health Perspectives*, April 2008, www.ehponline.org/members/2008/10912/ 10912.pdf.

18 DDT's effects on wildlife, widespread persistence in environment: *Silent Spring*, Rachel Carson, Cornell University Press, 1962, www.envirocancer.cornell.edu/FactSheet/Pesticide/fs2.ddt. cfm; University of Idaho, agls.uidaho.edu/etox/lectures/lecture02/Slides_SILENTSPRING.pdf.

18 DDT in Inuit breast milk: UN Environment Programme, www.chem.unep.ch/Pops/POPs_ Inc/ press_releases/pressrel-2k/pr24.htm.

18 DDT effects on children of exposed mothers: University of California, Davis, www.universityof california.edu/news/article/8291.

18 Young children's unsafe exposure to pesticides in food: EWG report, "How 'Bout Them Apples?" www.ewg.org/files/apples.pdf.

18 Extra nutritional benefits of organic produce: University of California, Davis, "Organic and Sustainable Foods Have More Polyphenolics Linked to Health Benefits," 2003, www.news.ucdavis.edu/search/news_detail.lasso?id=6312.

18 Largest organic study to date, in Britain, shows added antioxidants: www.timesonline.co.uk/tol/news/uk/health/article3753446.ece.; Organic adds nutritional boost equivalent to eating an extra portion of fruits and vegetables a day, says lead UK researcher Carlo Leifert, www.medicalnewstoday.com/articles/86972.php. Also see Organic Trade Association, www.ota.com/organic/benefits/nutrition.html.

19 Pesticides killing wild birds: Smithsonian Migratory Bird Center, www.nationalzoo.si.edu/ConservationAndScience/MigratoryBirds/Fact_Sheets/default.cfm?fxsht=8;

19 Pesticides killing wildlife: *Seattle Times* article, www.seattletimes.nwsource.com/html/localnews/2009097653_webpesticides21.html;

19 Pesticides killing beneficial insects: University of California, Davis, www.ipm.ucdavis.edu/QT/beneficialinsectscard.html.

19 Synthetic fertilizer runoff causing ocean dead zones: *Scientific American,* www.scientificamerican.com/article.cfm?id=oceanic-dead-zones-spread.

18–19 Various pesticides' toxicity to humans and wildlife, including amphibians, fish, and other aquatic life: See www.pesticideinfo.org and www.extoxnet.org searchable databases.

19 Organic farming methods: interviews with Bob Scowcroft, executive director, Organic Farming and Research Foundation, www.ofrf.org, and Frederick Kirschenmann, president, Stone Barns Center for Sustainable Agriculture, www.stonebarnscenter.org, former member National Organic Standards Board. Organic farming methods and standards are also summarized on the website of the Organic Trade Association, www.ota.org

19 Pollen drift from GMOs: A 2009 study found that genes from genetically modified corn had spread to wild corn, as reported in *New Scientist*, www.newscientist.com/article/mg20126964.200-transgenes-found-in-wild-corn.html.

19 Monsanto sues organic farmers for growing crops contaminated by gene drift from genetically modified crops grown with Monsanto patented seed: as reported in All Business, www.allbusiness.com/legal/1058704-1.html.

19 Creation of "superweeds" through gene drift: www.newscientist.com/article/dn1882-genetically modified-superweeds-not-uncommon.html.

19 Risk of plants with pharmacological properties getting into human food supply through drift from GM crops: Union of Concerned Scientists report, www.ucsusa.org/food_and_agriculture/science_and_impacts/impacts_genetic_engineering/how-does-seed-contamination.html.

19 GM crops fail to increase crop yields, as compared with traditional plant breeding: Union of Concerned Scientists report, www.ucsusa.org/food_and_agriculture/science_and_impacts /science/failure-to-yield.html.

20 Local foods and food miles: research by Leopold Institute for Sustainable Agriculture, Iowa State

University, www.leopold.iastate.edu/research/marketing.htm; and article in Slate, www.slate.com /id/2200202/pagenum/228-29.

20 Michael Pollan quote: Mindy Pennybacker, "Local or Organic? I'll Take Both," The Green Guide, Sept. 2006, www.e-greenguide.net/doc/116/local.

20 Local food marketplace and survival of diversified small family farms: American Farmland Trust, www.farmland.org/actioncenter/no-farms-no-food/local-food.

22 Protected Harvest label is a good example of IPM standards: Consumers Union Eco-Labels project, www.greenerchoices.org/eco-labels/label.cfm?LabelID=176&searchType=Label %20cate gory&searchValue=Pest%20Management%20&refpage=labelCategory&refqstr=labelCategory Name%3DPest%2520Management%2520UCS.

22 Transitional organic definition: www.edf.org/page.cfm?tagID=4549; tritrainingcenter.org/ course/.

23 Organic marketplace growth: www.ota.com/organic/mt/business.html.

23 Local foods marketplace growth: www.packagedfacts.com/about/release.asp?id=918.

24 A label to hope for: interview with Fred Kirschenman. "It's a values-based value chain, with full transparency, joining social and environmental standards," Kirschenman said about the new family farm label.

25 Marion Nestle, quoted in Mark Bittman, "Eating Food That's Better for You, Organic or Not," *New York Times*, March 22, 2009.

30 No added sulfites in U.S. organic wine: Mindy Pennybacker, "Uncork the Organic," The Green Guide, www.e-greenguide.net/doc/33/wine.

33 Organic beer loophole: Tom Daykin, "Homegrown Hops," *Milwaukee Journal Sentinel*, June 24, 2007, online at www.jsonline.com/business/29442239.html.

3. Fish

36 Smaller, younger fish have fewer pollutants: www.epa.gov/waterscience/fish/files/30 cwafish.pdf, and Rick Moonen, *Fish Without a Doubt*, Houghton Mifflin, 2008.

36–37 Vegetarian fish have fewer contaminants: www.ewg.org/node/16023.

36 Omega-3s in sardines, other fish: American Heart Association, "Fish and Omega-3 Fatty Acids," www.americanheart.org/presenter.jhtml?identifier=3048211, and Cheryl Redmond, "How to Shop for Heart Healthy Fish," *Natural Health Magazine*, May 2003, www.findarticles.com/p/arti cles/mi_m0NAH/is_4_33/ai_100732358/.

36 Tuna versus swordfish mercury calculations: based on FDA chart of mercury levels in fish by species, www.vm.cfsan.fda.gov/~frf/sea-mehg.html.

36, 44 Risk of nervous system harm and reduced IQ through PCB and mercury exposure in the womb when mother eats contaminated fish: Philip J. Landrigan, M.D., Herbert L. Needleman, M.D., and Mary Landrigan, M.P.A., *Raising Healthy Children in a Toxic World: 101 Smart Solutions for Every Family*, Rodale, 2001, pp. 57–58.

49 Wild-capture fisheries most damaging action in ocean: interview with Christopher Mann, director Pew Environment Group Campaign for Healthy Oceans.

49 Bycatch tons per year: United Nations, www.un.org/esa/sustdev/csd/bdoc99-6.pdf.

50 LAPPs, CSFs, other sustainable fishing partnerships between fishermen, consumers, and conservation groups: Environmental Defense Fund, www.edf.org.

50 Sustainable versus destructive fishing methods: www.edf.org and www.seaweb.org.

45 Number of times fish with low or moderate levels of mercury or PCBs can safely be eaten by women and children per week or month: Environmental Defense Fund Seafood Health Alert Chart, www.edf.org/page.cfm?tagID=17694; EPA and FDA joint advisory, www.cfsan.fda.gov; update, ewg.org/node/27431.

44 Dioxins in higher levels in farmed salmon: www.edf.org. To find health benefits of and contaminants in all kinds of fish, search by name in the "Find a Fish" section of the EDF Seafood Selector, www.edf.org/page.cfm?tagID=1540, or in the Monterey Bay Aquarium's Seafood Watch, www.mbayaq.org.

44 Nervous system and brain damage due to mercury exposure: Environmental Health News, www.environmentalhealthnews.org/ehs/newscience/low-mercury-levels-damage-nerves.

44 One in six U.S. babies born each year could be at risk of developmental harm due to mercury: *New York Times*, www.nytimes.com/2004/02/10/science/epa-raises-estimate-of-babies-affected-by-mercury-exposure.html?scp=1&sq=one%20in%20six%20u.s.%20newborns%20mercury%20exposure&st=cse.

44 Symptoms of mercury poisoning: Environmental Health Perspectives, www.ehponline.org/press/mercury.html; usatoday.com/news/health/2002-11-04-fish-1acover_x.htm, and sierraclub.org/mercury/health_effects/.

45 American women's mercury blood levels decrease: Environmental Health Perspectives, www.ehponline.org/members/2008/11674/11674.pdf.

44–45 Benefits of eating low-mercury fish outweigh risks: Babies of mothers who ate low-mercury fish had higher IQs in 2008 Harvard Medical School study; Team leader Dr. Emily Oken wrote that "Women should continue to eat fish—especially during pregnancy—but should choose fish types likely to be lower in mercury." From *Science Daily*, www.sciencedaily.com/releases/2008/09/080909205559.htm.

45 The odd bit of contaminated fish probably won't do you any harm: interview with Timothy Fitzgerald, scientist, oceans program, EDF.

49 Ninety percent of large predator fish disappearing: *Science News*, www.redorbit.com/news/science/2027/fish_are_fast_disappearing_from_oceans/.

51 Impact of industrial fish farming: www.edf.org/article.cfm?contentID=5323; and Pew Charitable Trusts' aquaculture report, www.pewtrusts.org/uploadedFiles/wwwpewtrustsorg/Reports/Protecting_ocean_life/Sustainable_Marine_Aquaculture_final_1_07.pdf.

4. Meat, Dairy, Poultry, and Eggs

55 U.S. longevity study: *Archives of Internal Medicine*, March 23, 2009, www.pubs.ama-assn.org/media/2009a/0323.dtl#1; German longevity study: www.dkfz.de/en/presse/pressemitteilungen/2005/dkfz_pm_05_26_e.php.

56–57 Greenhouse gas emissions saved by eating less meat: Replacing red meat for one day, or one seventh of your week's calories, with poultry, eggs, and fish, reduces greenhouse gases by 760 fewer miles per year. Substituting vegetables for one day equals driving 1,160 fewer miles per year. Carnegie Mellon study, "Food-Miles and the Relative Climate Impacts of Food Choices in the U.S.," Weber and Matthes, published in *Environmental Science and Technology* 42, no. 10 (April, 2008), www.pubs.acs.org/doi/abs/10.1021/es702969f.

57 Eating more fruits and vegetables relationship to weight loss: Centers for Disease Control, www.cdc.gov/nccdphp/dnpa/nutrition/pdf/rtp_practitioner_10_07.

57 Fewer heart attacks, stroke among those eating more fruits and vegetables: Harvard School of Public Health, www.hsph.harvard.edu/nutritionsource/what-should-you-eat/vegetablesfull -story/index.html.

56, 58 Water consumed in meat production: Worldwatch Institute, www.usc-online.ca/envirowest ern/EnviroTipsLinks/WorldWatchArticle.pdf.

56, 58 Water footprint of meat: Cornell University economist David Pimentel, www.books.google. com/books?id=yLmGPtZTHUYC&pg=PA72&lpg=PA72&dq=water+required+to+produce+ beef&source=web&ots=NDbGUIYwcz&sig=aiaEIi1t4Ekx_0cfiMjs5hgY6MU&hl=en&sa=X&oi= book_result&resnum=8&ct=result#PPA72,M1.

58 IPCC climate chair says to eat less meat: BBC News, www.news.bbc.co.uk/1/hi/sci/tech/ 7600005.stm.

60 USDA process verified grass-fed label: www.greenerchoices.org/eco-labels/label.cfm?Label ID=303&searchType=Label&searchValue=grassfed&refpage=labelSearch&refqstr=label%3Dgras sfedmotherearthnews.com/Sustainable-Farming/2008-04-01/USDA-Grass-Fed-Label. aspx.

61 Antibiotics fed to livestock: www.scientificamerican.com/article.cfm?id=most-us-antibiotics -fed-t environmentalhealthnews.org/ehs/news/antibiotics-in-crops.

63 Recombinant bovine growth hormone (rBGH) in milk: www.foodandwaterwatch.org/food/food safety/dairy/what-research-shows.

63 Big milk companies banning use of rBGH in dairy cows: www.usatoday.com/money/industries/ food/2009-03-15-dairy-growth-hormone-ban_N.htm.

5. Food Storage and Cookware

64, 70, 71 Microwaving in plastic: www.greenerpenny.blogspot.com/2008/11/use-glass-instead-of- microwave-safe.html.

66 Phthalates's detrimental effects on human male reproductive development: Main et al., "Human breast milk contamination with phthalates and alterations of endogenous reproductive hormones in infants three months old," Environmental *Health Perspectives*, www.ehponline.org/docs/2005/ 8075/abstract.html.

69 "Sex and plastic": Mark Schapiro, *Exposed: The Toxic Chemistry of Everyday Products and What's at Stake for American Power*, Chelsea Green, 2007, pp. 53–54.

69 Phthalates's association with changes in reproductive hormones and increased allergies in infants

and children, and with changes in sperm quality in men: Luz Claudio and Reeve Chace, "Quick Guide to Plastics," *Mount Sinai Community Health Bulletin*, June 2006.

71, 72 Bioplastics require industrial or municipal composting, will not biodegrade in home composting bins or piles: Bioplastics Institute, www.bpiworld.org/BPI-Public/Program/FAQ.html; world centric.org/about-us/faq#general5.

74 BPA in cans: www.ewg.org/reports/bpatimeline.

75 Nonstick chemicals and infertility, flu symptoms, other scientific studies: summarized by Environmental Working Group, www.ewg.org/node/27570.

76 Environmental Protection Agency warnings on PFOA: www.epa.gov/oppt/pfoa/.

6. Appliances

81 Cold water wash saves 90 percent energy: Department of Energy, www.1.eere.energy.gov/consumer/tips/laundry.html.

81–82 Energy and carbon saved by washing four out of five loads in cold water: Center for a New American Dream, www.c3.newdream.org/.

82–83 GHG emissions savings from line-drying, cold-water wash, and other household uses: Environmental Protection Agency, www.epa.gov/climatechange/emissions/ind_assumptions.htmlaceee. org; and Emily Main and Paul McRandle, "A Calculated Loss: How to Reduce Your Global Warming Emissions," The Green Guide, March 2007, www.e-greenguide.net/doc/119/calculator.

82–83 Line-drying and alarm clock: Stanford University, www.sustainableStanford.edu.

85 EPA classifies GHG as pollutants, threat to health: www.washingtonpost.com/wpdyn/content/article/2009/04/17/AR2009041701453.html.

85 Climate change is a deadly and worsening public health issue: Dr. Howard Frumkin, director of the U.S. Centers for Disease Control's National Center for Environmental Health, and Dr. Jonathan Patz, University of Wisconsin health sciences professor, at the annual meeting of the American Public Health Association in 2007. The World Health Organization estimated that 160,000 people died in 2000 from malaria, diarrhea, malnutrition, and drownings from floods—problems that public health and climate scientists contend were worsened by global warming. "Scientists suggest cutting calories and carbon dioxide could help save lives and the planet," by Seth Borenstein, AP science writer, Nov. 11, 2007, in the *Seattle Times*, online at www./seattletimes.nwsource.com/html/nationworld/2004007857_webglobalwarmingdiet11.html.

86 Residential energy and other sectors' share of energy use, greenhouse gas emissions: Pew Environment, www.pewtrusts.org/news_room_detail.aspx?id=19520chart, and DOE, 1.eere.energy.gov/consumer/tips/home_energy.html.

84 McKinsey "low-hanging fruit" energy efficiency report: www.mckinsey.com/mgi/reports/pdfs/wasted_energy/MGI_wasted_energy.pdf.

87–88 Energy savings with Energy Star appliances: www.energystar.gov.

87–88 Washer/dryer green buying guide: www.greenerchoices.org/printProduct.cfm? product=washer; www.consumerreports.org/cro/appliances/laundry-and-cleaning/washing-machines/washing machine-recommendations/washing-machine.htm.

86 Carbon saved with laundry machine use tips, other home appliance, heating/cooling energy-saving tips: www.greenerchoices.org/globalwarmingsavecarbon.cfm, and www.aceee.org; www.greenerchoices.org/globalwarmingathome.cfm; and www.aceee.org/consumerguide/laundry.htm#newdryer. Also www.consumerreports.org/cro/appliances/laundry-and-cleaning/clothes-dryers/clothes-dryer-guide/features/clothes-dryers-features.htm.

88 Amount Americans saved in 2007 on their utility bills while reducing GHG emissions equal to those from 27 million vehicles: www.energystar.gov.

89 Also see EDF guide: www.fightglobalwarming.com/documents/5119_LowCarbonguide.pdf.

7. Lighting

91–94 CFL attributes, statistics, info: www.energystar.gov/index.cfm?c=cfls.pr_cfls.

91–98 LED attributes, statistics, residential lighting info: www.energystar.gov/index.cfm?c=ssl.pr_residential.

94 New crop of home lighting LEDs: www.newscientist.com/article/dn16496-cheap-superefficient-led-lights-on-the-horizon.html.

94 Incandescents release 90 percent of their energy as heat; CFLs 30 percent: www.gelighting.com.

94 Money and carbon savings: www.energystar.gov.

94 CFL carbon savings: www.nrdc.org.

94 McKinsey, payback from CFLs: www.mckinsey.com/mgi/reports/pdfs/wasted_energy/MGI_wasted_energy.pdf.

95 CFLs and mercury: www.energystar.gov/index.cfm?c=cfls.pr_cfls_mercury.

95 Some manufacturers are voluntarily using less mercury than EPA allowances: Environmental Working Group reports, December 2008; www.ewg.org/reports/compact-fluorescent-light-bulbs.

96–97 Top CFL light quality picks: based on personal tests of different bulbs with varying CRIs.

98 LEDs will grow to 70 percent of the lighting market and save Americans $280 billion over the next 20 years: Jim Brodrick, lighting manager for the U.S. Department of Energy, in "Bright Future: Thanks to Improved Technology, LEDs May Be Ready to Take Off," by Sari Krieger, *Wall Street Journal*, Sept. 15, 2008. Krieger also quotes lighting industry sources and public officials, who say LEDs, which use an average 85 percent less energy and last 30 times longer than incandescents, and use about half as much energy and last five times longer than CFLs, will become the standard lighting choice.

99 Quick Home Energy Checklist: Heating, cooling, appliance proportion of energy use in average home, www.1.eere.energy.gov/consumer/tips/home_energy.html; chart of different appliances' energy consumption, www.1.eere.energy.gov/consumer/tips/appliances.html.

99 Turning thermostat up (summer) and down (winter) for savings: www.e-greenguide.net/doc/119/calculator; greenerchoices.org/globalwarmingsavecarbon.cfm.

99–100 Refrigerator and stovetop energy savings tips: Mindy Pennybacker, "The Cooler Kitchen," *E. Magazine*, Jan. 2008; ACEEE Consumer Guide to Home Energy Savings, www.aceee.org. Keep your fridge nice and full; less energy will be wasted. An old fridge can cost you up to $208; www.consumerenergycenter.org/home/appliances/refrigerators.html.

104 Defeating energy "vampires": up to 75 percent of power from electronics and appliances drawn when they're not running, www.energy.gov/applianceselectronics.htm.

104 Plugging electronics into power strips and turning off overnight; unplugging small appliances from wall socket: www.eia.doe.gov/kids/classactivities/energyarticles.html#energyvampires.

104 Watts saved with computer on "sleep" mode, and how to activate it: www.blogs.consumerre ports.org/electronics/news/.

105 Green computer ratings: energy use, longevity, recyclability, toxic components, lifecycle impact, www.epeat.net (EPEAT's criteria include Energy Star, www.energystar.gov).

106 Cell phone, computer, electronic game console makers: electronics companies green report card for product lifecycles, including energy and materials used in production, recyclability of product, www.greenpeace.org/usa/press-center/reports4/guide-to-greener-electronics-11.

8. Saving Water

109 Seventy-five percent of home water use is in bathroom: California Energy Commission, www.energy.ca.gov.

110 Which uses more water?: www.blogs.consumerreports.org/home/2008/08/shower-or-bath.html.

111 Better for You: www.skincarephysicians.com/agingskinnet/winter_skin.html; www.everyday health.com/skin-and-beauty/loving-care-for-dry-skin.aspx

111 Planet's limited available fresh water: www.globalchange.umich.edu/globalchange2/current/lectures/freshwater_supply/freshwater.html.

110–13 Showers are responsible for about 17 percent of residential indoor water use in the United States, and Water Sense efficiency standards are being developed for showerheads: www.epa.gov /watersense/pp/showerheads.htm. At press date, Water Sense labels could be found on faucets and faucet aerators, www.epa.gov/watersense/pp/bathroom_faucets.htm, as well as on high-effi ciency toilets, www.epa.gov/watersense/pp/het.htm.

110–13 Water use statistics and water-saving tips are provided by The Alliance for Water Efficiency, www.allianceforwaterefficiency.org. Other good home water-saving tips can be found at www.cru. cahe.wsu.edu/CEPublications/eb0732/eb0732.pdf.

110–14 Hot water thermostat: www.greenerchoices.org/globalwarmingsavecarbon.cfm.

114 Toilet stats: www.epa.gov/watersense.

9: Simple Green Housekeeping

117–18 Cleaning products leading cause of calls to poison control centers: American Association of Poison Control Centers, www.aapcc.org.

119 Household cleaning ingredients to avoid: Pamela Lundquist, "Spring Cleaning," The Green Guide, May 2002, www.e-greenguide.net/doc/90/lundquist2.

124 Women and the environment report: www.womenandenvironment.org/campaignsandprograms /SafeCleaning/HazardsReport.pdf.

119 Problems of antibacterial soaps with triclosan: www.worldwatch.org/node/1501.

120 Household cleaning chemicals and breathing problems studies: California Air Resources Board, www.arb.ca.gov/research/indoor/INDOOR.HTM; www.arb.ca.gov/research/indoor/cleaning_products_fact_sheet-10-2008.

120 Regular home use of spray cleaners and air fresheners was associated with a 30–50 percent higher risk of asthma symptoms: 2007 study in the *American Journal of Respiratory and Critical Care* medicine, online at www.ajrccm.atsjournals.org/cgi/content/abstract/176/8/735.

119, 120 Study of terpenes and glycol ethers: www.arb.ca.gov/research/abstracts/01-336.htm.

120 Cleaning chemicals harming aquatic life downstream: www.sierraclub.org/toxics/nonylphenol_ethoxylates3.pdf.

120 Phosphorous and ammonia from cleaning products cause oxygen depletion in streams, lakes: www.pubs.usgs.gov/circ/circ1136/circ1136.html.

125 Disinfecting toilet seat and other surfaces: Hydrogen peroxide is an effective and least-toxic germ killer used as the active ingredient by Seventh Generation in its disinfectants, according to Martin Wolf, the company's director of product quality and technology.

125 Hydrogen peroxide also registered as a microbial pesticide by the EPA: www.epa.gov/pesticides/factsheets/chemicals/hydrogenperoxide_peroxyaceticacid_factsheet.htm#bkmrk4.

124 White vinegar and baking soda killed 90 percent of microbes linked to infectious diseases, including staphylococcus, salmonella, E. coli, and even poliovirus, while chlorine bleach and Lysol disinfectant spray killed 99.9 percent: Although the stronger chemicals worked better, University of North Carolina researchers said this did not mean that microbes on home surfaces transmitted infection or whether kissing, touching, and sharing eating utensils among family members were more to blame, www.unc.edu/news/archives/jan00/rutala012100.htm.

124 VOCs in vinyl: www.plentymag.com/events/2008/06/shower_curtains_without_that_t.php; www.womenandenvironment.org/pdf/VolatileVinyl.pdf. Federal legislation banning phthalates in mattresses, toys, other children's products: www.consumersunion.org/pub/core_product_safety/005925.html. www.ombwatch.org/article/articleview/4316/1/544; www.washingtonpost.com/wp-dyn/content/article/2008/08/01/AR2008080103007.html.

126 VOCs in pesticides: National Institutes of Health, www.pubmedcentral.nih.gov/articlerender.fcgi?artid=1241309.

126 Health effects of pesticides in indoor air: Lower birth weights and smaller head circumferences were found in infants of mothers exposed to the most indoor residential pesticides when pregnant, studies by the Columbia University Center for Children's Environmental Health, led by Frederica Perera, published in the March and May 2004 issues of *Environmental Health Perspectives*; early exposure to household insecticides linked to higher risk of childhood leukemia, Ma et al., *Environmental Health Perspectives*, Sept. 2002.

127 VOCs from flame retardants: PBDEs and learning problems, www.e-greenguide.net/doc/109/pbde; e-greenguide.net/doc/97/pbde.

129–130 Formaldehyde offgassing from pressed woods and fabric treatments: California Air Resources Board, www.arb.ca.gov/research/indoor/formaldGL08-04.pdf.

131 VOCs evaporating from paints: Worldwatch Institute, www.worldwatch.org/node/1496.

132 Concentrated detergent: *New York Times* article, Jan. 25, 2009, www.nytimes.com/2009/01/25/business/25walmart.html?pagewanted=3&_r=1&emc=eta1.

133 Laundry ingredients to watch out for: Women's Voices for the Environment, www.womenandenvironment.org/campaignsandprograms/SafeCleaning/HazardsReport.pdf.

137–139 Dry cleaning: www.epa.gov/dfe/pubs/garment/ctsa/factsheet/ctsafaq.htm coalitionforcleanair.org.

10. Reduce, Reuse, Recycle

141 Green savings from paying bills online: www.electronicpayments.org/pdfs/EnvironmentalImpactsStudy_09-19.pdf.

142, 144 Junk mail stats: www.nativeforest.org/stop_junk_mail/nfn_junk_mail_guide.htm.

148 Only 10 percent of U.S. cell phones are recycled: www.epa.gov/epawaste/partnerships/plugin/cellphone/index.htmII.

148 Recycling cell phones: www.epa.gov/epawaste/conserve/materials/ecycling/faq.htm#cellbenefits.

11. Skin and Hair

154–55 Fragrance and phthalates: Campaign for Safe Cosmetics "Not Too Pretty" report, www.safecosmetics.org/downloads/A%20Little%20Prettier%20report.pdfsciencedirect.com/science?_ob=ArticleURL&_udi=B6T6D-4CJXWH0-1&_user=10&_rdoc=1&_fmt=&_orig=search&_sort=d&view=c&_acct=C000050221&_version=1&_urlVersion=0&_userid=10&md5=0aed7e7445ec678cbc2d7ad17f975ec4.

156 Phthalates and lower sperm quality: *Environmental Health Perspectives*, www.ehponline.org/docs/2008/11146/abstract.html; www.ehponline.org/docs/2005/8100/abstract.html. www.ourstolenfuture.org/NewScience/oncompounds/phthalates/2006/2006-1101 hauseretal.html.

156–57 Phthalates affect fish: 2004 study, *Newsweek* article, at www.lists.dep.state.fl.us/pipermail/pharmwaste/2007-May/001166.html, and throughout chapter.

163_64 "Lose It" Personal Care Labels: www.greenerchoices.org/eco-labels/reportLabelCategory.cfm? labelCategoryName=General%20Claims&mode=view.

158–60 "Filthy Fifteen" ingredients list: Environmental Working Group and Campaign for Safe Cosmetics database, www.cosmeticsdatabase.com; interviews with EWG scientist Olga Naidenko and senior analyst Sean Gray; interview with Stacy Malkan, author of *Not Just a Pretty Face: The Ugly Side of the Beauty Industry* (New Society, 2007); website of the Organic Consumers Association, www.organicconsumers.org.

159 Definition of ethoxylation: www.answers.com/topic/ethoxylation.

163–64 Beauty Seals Chart: conversations with David Bronner and Stacy Malkan.

164 NSF/ANSI standard adopted in United States: www.naturalproductsmarketplace.com/hotnews/nsf-releases-organic-personal-care-standard.html; www.organicconsumers.org/bodycare/drb_compare.cfm.

163 Terrachoice greenwashing study: www.terrachoice.com/files/6_sins.pdf.

169 Natural preservatives list: *Ecologist Magazine*, www.theecologist.org/pages/archive_detail.asp?content_id=1197&j=y.

170 Parabens and breast cancer.

172 Oxybenzone/benzophenone 3 linked to hormone disruption: Environmental Health Perspectives, www.ehponline.org/members/2008/11269/11269.html; Oxybenzone toxicity: www.ewg.org/node/26212.

173 Nanoparticles: www.environmentalhealthnews.org/ehs/newscience/toxic-nanoparticles-get-into-cells/.

182 Deodorant and parabens: National Institutes of Health publication on breast cancer, www.ncbi.nlm.nih.gov/pubmed/14745841?dopt=abstract. EWG Safe Cosmetics Database, www.safecosmeticsdatabase.com; Breast cancer fund, www.breastcancerfund.org; Breast Cancer Action, www.breastcanceraction.org.

184 1, 4 Dioxane: California attorney general files lawsuit against organic-labeled cosmetic companies for contamination with 1.4 dioxane, 2008, www.organicconsumers.org; www.safecosmetics.live.radicaldesigns.org///article.php?id=221.

185 Triclosan: *Worldwatch State of the World 2004*, "Antibacterial Soaps," Mindy Pennybacker, www.books.google.com/books?id=-j2ni69-Rm8C&pg=PA67&lpg=PA67&dq=american+medical+association+advises+against+home+antibacterial+cleaners&source=web&ots=5QgHfvnFpn&sig=s3oyHulTDoEuGP1GjQO3EgjC8B8&hl=en&sa=X&oi=book_result&resnum=10&ct=result#PPA67,M1.

12: Clothing

188, 190 Chemicals used for cotton T-shirts, cotton statistics: Pesticides Action Network, www.panna.org; cotton T-shirt takes 700 gallons and a pair of Levi's stonewashed jeans take 500 gallons, according to the Wall Street Journal, Feb. 17, 2009.

190 Recycled clothing energy saved: www.patagonia.com.

191–95 Fibers' green life cycles: www.worldwatch.org worldwatch.org/node/1485. ("Good Stuff" consumer products section, clothing), and *Worldwatch State of the World 2004*, cotton T-shirt chapter; rayon (www.fibersource.com/F-TUTOR/rayon.htm); bamboo (www.organicclothing.blogs.com/my_weblog/2008/08/bamboo-sprouting-green-myths.html); critique of bamboo/shady origins (www.bamboosa.com/bamboo.php?PID=63 [processing, certifications]; Tencell (www.organicclothing.blogs.com/my_weblog/2005/11/tencel_sustaina.html); how lyocell is processed.

190–95 Comparative lifecycles (energy, materials, pollution) of polyester, hemp, cotton, organic hemp, organic cotton, "Ecological Footprint and Water Analysis of Cotton, Hemp and Polyester," by Nia Cherret for the Bioregional Development Group and World Wildlife Fund, including where made/grown and processed in 2005 study: www.organicexchange.org/Farm/Reading %20and %20References/Cotton%20Hemp%20Polyester%20study%20SEI%20and%20Bioregional%20and %20WWF%20Wales.pdf.

196–98 Finishes and dyes: PFOA in fabric finishes, www.epa.gov/nheerl/rtd/rtd_perf.html; ewg.org; fabric treatments and dyes: www.thegreenguide.com; "Waste Couture: Environmental Impact of the Clothing Industry," Luz Claudio, Environmental Health Perspectives, http://www.ehponline. org/realfiles/docs/2007/115-9/focus-abs.html volume 115k.

200 International Marketecology Organization (IMO) certifies organic and fair trade, and eco-sounder forestry and textile products: Organic Trade Association "Organic Pages," www.ota.org.

200 Fair trade: www.coopamerica.org/programs/sweatshops/sweatfreeproducts.cfm, notes on FLA.

209 Toys: www.greenpeace.org/usa/news/toy-report card; phthalates banned in children's products, including toys, by U.S. Congress, 2008, www.newsweek.com/id/150342.

13. Walking, Biking, and Ride Sharing

215 If every American between the ages of 10 and 74 years spent 30 minutes per day walking or cycling instead of driving, we'd cut CO_2 emissions by 64 million tons—about the total amount released by the State of New Mexico every year—save 6.5 billion tons of gasoline, and lose 3 billion tons of excess body weight, according to 2005 research by Paul Higgins, a scientist at the American Meteorological Society. By walking an extra half hour a day, you, alone, could lose 13 pounds a year: "Scientists suggest cutting calories and carbon dioxide could help save lives and the planet," Seth Borenstein, AP science writer, Nov. 11, 2007, in the *Seattle Times*, www./seattle times.nwsource.com/html/nationworld/2004007857_webglobalwarmingdiet11.html.

216 Air versus car travel cross-country: Emily Main and Paul McRandle, "A Calculated Loss: How to Reduce Your Global Warming Emissions," The Green Guide, March 2007. Bob Schildgen attributes even fewer carbon emissions per air passenger in his book *Hey, Mr. Green* (Sierra Club, 2008).

222 23 Carbon weight loss chart: The Green Guide (see previous note), and www.epa.gov/climate change/emissions/ind_calculator.html.

224 Carbon offset companies ratings: www.cleanair-coolplanet.org/consumersguidetocarbonoff sets.pdf; "Voluntary offsets for air-travel carbon emissions," www.tufts.edu/tie/tci/pdf/tci_car bon_offsets.

ABOUT THE AUTHOR

MINDY PENNYBACKER, editor and founder of *www.GreenerPenny.com*, was editor-in-chief of *The Green Guide* for over a decade, as well as cofounder of *thegreenguide.com*. She has worked with such organizations as The Trust for Public Land, The Natural Resources Defense Council (NRDC), and Mothers & Others for a Livable Planet. Recipient of a Stegner Fellowship and a National Endowment for the Arts Award for her writing, her work has appeared in *The New York Times*, *The Atlantic Monthly*, *Sierra*, and *The Nation*, among others.

An ardent surfer and consumer advocate, Mindy graduated from Stanford, The Iowa Writers' Workshop, and UC Davis School of Law. After twenty-six years in New York City, she has returned to Honolulu, her birthplace.

This book grew out of her long-standing commitment to answering readers' questions about green living.

ABOUT THE ILLUSTRATOR

CAROLYN VIBBERT is the award-winning illustrator of *Do One Green Thing*. Her richly detailed pen-and-ink drawings combine a graphic sensibility with strong traditional technique. Carolyn's work has been featured in a variety of mediums, from product labels to books and interactive projects. A former designer for Hallmark, her commercial clients now include Frito-Lay, Coors, Quaker, Williams-Sonoma, Pottery Barn, Cakebread Cellars, Ghirardelli, Time, and Chronicle Books.

After graduating from Virginia Commonwealth University, Carolyn lived and worked in San Francisco, Seattle, Washington, D.C., and Kansas City. She and her husband, John, have finally settled down in the historic seaside town of Portsmouth, New Hampshire, along with their feline companion, Sube.

Index

children eating, 40, 44–45, 53

choose it/lose it, canned, 47–48

choose it/lose it, eating, 38–39

choose it/lose it, environment of, 47–48

choose it/lose it, for health, 41–43

choose it/lose it, methods, 50

destruction of, 49

dioxins in, 39

eating frequency of, 40

eating smaller, 34–36, 40

Energy Star label for, 45

for health, 36

industrial, farming, 51

large, wild, 49

locally caught, 52

mercury in, 36, 39–45, 48

NPE in, 120

One Green Thing, 34

PCBs in, 39–45

polluted, 36

resources, 228–29

safest, 36–37

sardines, 35–36

Fitzgerald, Timothy, 45

floor cleaner, 124

food, xiv. *See also* containers, food; organic

BPA in canned, 74–75

fair traded, xv

health science plastic on, 69

Iowa travels of, 20

junk, 25

labels, 22

miles, 24, 238

One Green Thing, 15

pesticides in, 18

processed, 25–26

resources for, 226–28

seasonal, website finding, 24

food, local/heritage, xi, xiv, xv, xvii, 15

benefits of, 20

growth of, 23

resources for, 228

food, sustainably grown. *See also* organic

choose it/lose it, produce, 16–17

finding, 227

Food Alliance Certified, 59, 62

website of, 22

Food and Drug Administration (FDA), 165, 166

fish guidelines from, 45

Food Politics (Nestle), 25

foodshed, 238

Forest Stewardship Council (FSC), 74

toys certified by, 209

wood standards of, 130

formaldehyde, 128, 159

in carpets/pressed

woods, 129–30

dangers of, 129

fabric releasing, 196

synthetics using, 198

fossil fuels, 112

cars powered by, 216, 218

plastic bottles using, 3

synthetic chemical using, 19

fragrance, 159, 183

allergic reactions to, 156

choose it/lose it, personal care, 155

One Green Thing, 153–54

phthalates in, 153–57

synthetic, 153–54

free range, ix

Frumkin, Howard, 247*n*85

FSC. *See* Forest Stewardship Council

fume-free oven cleaner, 123

furniture, pressed wood

formaldehyde in, 129–30

green sources of, 130

G

gas, natural, 85–86

GE/GM. *See* genetic engineering/genetic modification

gene splicing. *See* genetic engineering/genetic modification

General Mills, 63

genetic engineering/genetic

"How to Go Green in Hard Times," 112
hydrogen peroxide, 250n125

I

IARC. *See* International Agency for Research on Cancer
IFOA. *See* International Federation of Organic Agricultural Movements
IKEA, 95, 126, 209
In Defense of Food (Pollan), 20
ingeo, 192
Ingredients to Look for/Avoid, xviii
insecticides, 126, 242n18
Integrated Pest Management (IPM), 23, 27, 127
    websites of, 22
International Agency for Research on Cancer (IARC), 137
International Federation of Organic Agricultural Movements (IFOAM), 192
International Panel on Climate Change (IPCC), 58, 111
Iowa State University, 20
IPCC. *See* International Panel on Climate Change

K

kilowatt hour (kWh), 239
Kmart, 199
kWh. *See* kilowatt hour

L

labels/seals, xviii, 17, 20, 21, 128
    choose it/lose it, household cleaning, 135
    choose it/lose it, meat, 59–60
    choose it/lose it , cosmetics, 162–65
    composting, 72
    eco, 30–31
    Ecologo, 163
    egg/dairy, 62
    EPA, 87
    fair trade, 200
    family farm, 24
    ingredients on, 154–55
    international organic, 192
    junk food, 25
    nanoparticles, 162
    "natural" on, 154
    organic, 17, 20, 23, 26
    produce, 22
    seafood, 229
    third-party verified, 59–60
LAPPs. *See* Limited Access

Privilege Programs
laundry, 223
    choose it/lose it, detergent, 133
    choose it/lose it, energy-efficient machines for, 84
    cold water for, 81–82
    costs of, 86
    delicate, 138
    detergent, 132–36
    dryers, 87–88
    efficient washers for, 87–88
    energy tips for, 84
    hang to dry, 82–83
    One Green Thing, 81–83, 132
    shopping tips for, 87–89
LDPE #4. *See* low-density polyethylene
lead, 5, 106, 159
    testing water for, 6–7
    toys with, 209
LEDs. *See* light-emitting diodes
Leopold Institute for Sustainable Agriculture, 20
Lexan. *See* polycarbonate (PC #7)
"Lightbulb Campaign" website, 237
light-emitting diodes (LEDs), 239, 248n98
    choosing, 96, 98
    color of, 93